"Jennifer's voice—so wise, so real, so fierce, and so gentle—rings like a clear morning bell throughout each part of the book. When she is telling her own story, the bell is courageous; when she is giving instructions for a healthier, happier life, the bell is startling—it wakes you up; and when she is telling the deep and sometimes bewildering story of women's lives at the start of the 21st century, the bell rings with an original and beautiful sound. I think it's the sound of truth. I know the book will bring clarity and solace."

Elizabeth Lesser, author of *The New American Spirituality*

———

"The Comfort Queen's down-to-earth words guide women in how to take ourselves seriously enough to create the life we live while never taking ourselves so seriously that we cannot tenderly laugh at our own foibles. Openhearted wisdom for every woman who wants to live and love and laugh more fully."

Oriah Mountain Dreamer, author of *The Invitation*

———

"A delightful soul-searching exploration for all of us!"

Kay Allenbaugh, author of *Chocolate for a Woman's Soul*

———

"In a lighthearted and generous voice, Jennifer Louden provides a profound yet simple path for following your heart home."

Marcia Wieder, author of *Making Your Dreams Come True*

———

"Sassy, poignant, and smart, Louden's Comfort Queen places the source of a healthy, creative, balanced life exactly where it should be—in a woman's inner life. Instead of trying to change and control everything around her, Louden correctly says a woman should listen to her own Comfort Queen voice that knows what she needs. Using herself as a model, Louden entertains the reader as she teaches her, a winning combination."

Virginia Beane Rutter, author of *Embracing Persephone* and *Celebrating Girls*

———

"Jennifer Louden, in her lyrical style and intimate manner, encourages you to ask yourself the ultimate question: How conscious am I willing to be? This is a must-read for anyone ready to be accountable to life."

Connie Cockrell Kaplan, author of *The Woman's Book of Dreams*

———

The Comfort Queen's Guide to Life

Also by Jennifer Louden

The Woman's Comfort Book
The Couple's Comfort Book
The Pregnant Woman's Comfort Book
The Little Book of Sensual Comfort
The Woman's Retreat Book

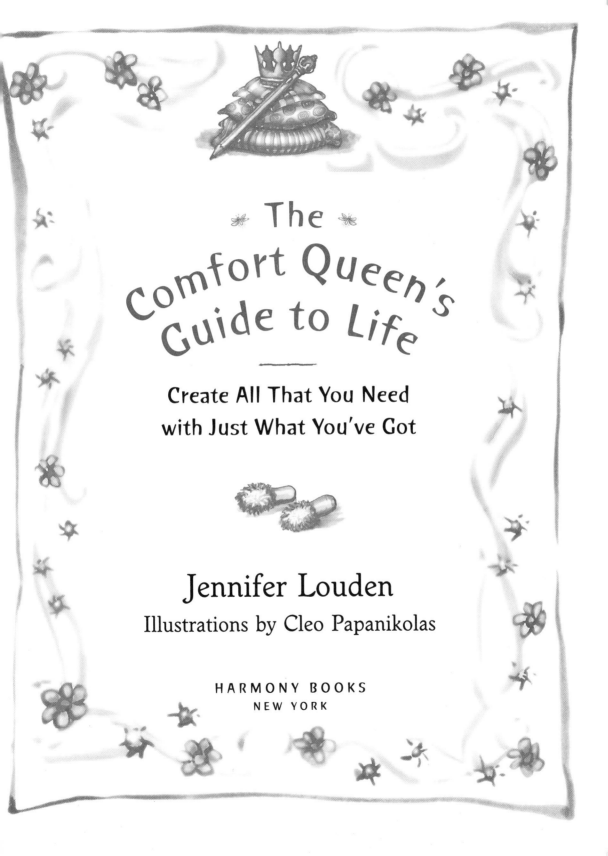

The
Comfort Queen's Guide to Life

Create All That You Need
with Just What You've Got

Jennifer Louden

Illustrations by Cleo Papanikolas

HARMONY BOOKS
NEW YORK

Published by Harmony Books, New York. Member of the Crown Publishing Group.

Random House, Inc. New York, Toronto, London, Sydney, Auckland

www.randomhouse.com

Harmony Books is a registered trademark and the Harmony Books colophon is a trademark of Random House, Inc.

Printed in the United States of America

Design by Lindgren/Fuller Design

Library of Congress Cataloging-in-Publication Data

Louden, Jennifer.
    The comfort queen's guide to life: create all that you need with just what you've got / by Jennifer Louden.—1st ed.
    1. Conduct of life.   2. Spiritual life.   I. Title.

BF637.C5 L675 2000
158.1—dc21

99-058209

ISBN 0-609-60527-5

First Edition

For Doyle Louden, my father,
who definitely creates his own life

Acknowledgments

All the women and men listed below have contributed to whatever is good and useful in this book; its oversights and crazy cracks are entirely my own.

Marcie Telander, you have provided me with sanctuary and guidance at two critical junctures in my life. You are a mentor and matchmaker: without you, I doubt I would have met CQ. Mark, thanks for your tender, loving pork roast and conversation. And Ranger, honey, you have my true love forever.

The wise books written by Carol Flinders, Marion Woodman, Stephanie Dowrick, Sue Monk Kidd, Caroline Casey, and Robert Johnson were of immeasurable help in my quest.

For letting me interview you and learn from your wisdom, for sending me your Comfort Queen stories, reading drafts of the book, or for trying out versions of the journal pages over the years, I send bushels of thanks to: Carolyn Atkinson, Jennifer Freed, Monica Relph-Whikman, Rachel Bagby, Beth Wilson, Kim Shiffer, Nicole Barnbe, Monica Fehlman, Mary Davies, Rose Hannah, Carol Blotter, Carol Floyd, Catherine Schmidt, Carol Benn, Bernadette Coffey, Ellen, Ashley, Andrea Sharman, Vicki Capestany, Debbie Tripp, Trace-Ann Green, Linda Jackman, Tiffany Tholmes, Taffy Hill, Susan Miller, Sheila Herrin, Sharina Adkins, Susan Erickson, Robin Galguera, Kim Rodeffer Funk, Molly J. McGarvey, Dawn Epstein, Lynn O'Keefe, Lynda Gross, Diana Lieffring, Sibel Golden, Kris Monka, Jody Thomas, Deborah Smith, Jodie Ireland, Linda Mattis, Ann Allen, Nora Gallagher, Saral Burdette, Audrey Berman, Beth Leonard, Kathy Richards, Deborah Smith, Janet Mauck, Domenica Bianca, Elia Wise, Kristina Coggins, Lori Couihan Childs, Maureen Murdock, Pat Pasick, Anna Bunting, Mary Judge, Katherine Morrow, Carol Kinsey, Michele Louden, Betty Louden, Randi Ragan, Paula Steinmetz,

Zuleikha, Maria Harris, Sandy Ingerman, Valerie Atcheson, Susan Gardiner, Susan Woolridge, Priscilla Stuckey, Janine Rood, Joanne Kinnaird, Elizabeth Densley, Patrizia Clerico, Rhonda Mitchell, Denise Icard, Louise Stone, and Susan Kaufmann.

For generously sharing your talent and your wily, down-to-earth mind, Cleo Papanikolas, thank you. You are a wondrous artist, and this book is so much more because of your contribution.

To my women's group, as we close in on five years, you continue to anchor me and constantly remind me to stop kvetching and start remembering what a lucky gal I am.

To Patty Gift: how refreshing to find someone in the corporate publishing maze that practices many of the principles she publishes. Thanks for your commitment and calm finesse. Kristen Wolfe and Kieran O'Brien, for attending to all the details and being patient with my scattered self, bless you. Tina Constable, Andrew Martin, Debbie Koenig, Andrea Rosen, Kim Robles, Lauren Dong, and Laura Duffy, crates of credit for your honest, can-do attitude.

Linda Loewenthal and Joan DeMayo, you're both Comfort Queens in my book. My neurotic self thanks you for the extra attention and hand-holding.

Barbara Moulton, our paths are again profoundly intertwined. Your loyalty and patience during my pit tenure was a lifeline that kept reminding me that it was indeed my name on the spine of those other books. Candace Groskreutz, thanks for braving the world of foreign rights and doing it so well. Anmarie Linsley, it's great working with someone who talks as fast as I do and gets the job done so well.

To Chris and Lilly, you are racking up big-time karmic points this time around—living with a writer is a special kind of penance, that's for sure. I love you both so.

Dad, finally you get a book dedicated to you! You continue to be an inspiration to me and to hold my hand when I doubt and stumble. Thank you. And you, too, Mom!

Contents

The Comfort Queen's Guide to Life

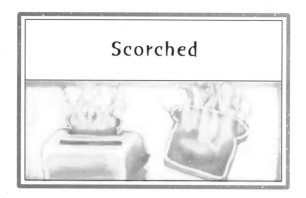

Scorched

I'm in Massachusetts to offer a workshop to women on self-care and self-nurturing. I almost turned down the event because I felt so disembodied from the material I have been talking and writing about for nine years. I'm cavernous inside, a ramshackle soul. The only way I nurture myself these days is by eating chocolate and whining, and even those are failing me.

It has become very apparent to me that I am spiritually disheveled. Half a bubble off plumb. Ravished and rattled, seriously scorched. My writing has floundered, my marriage is husk-like and brittle, my health hazy. The worst of it is that nothing tragic or even very bad has happened. No one has died, except my dog, Atticus. No one has lost their job. True, I'm not earning much money, and I'm very worried about that, but it feels more like a symptom than the disease itself. My life resembles a mudflat at low tide on a white-hot August day, and I'm very far from solid ground.

A friend recently told me the story of a shanachie, a Celtic storyteller. When a shanachie has either forgotten a story, not remembered all its parts, or bored her audience, she goes to the nearest crossroad and lies down with a stone on her stomach until she creates a new, more meaningful story. She lies in the middle of the road, people driving their sheep around her, stepping over her. They know what she is doing and they leave her alone. They even honor her: "Oh, there's a woman with a stone on her belly, mumbling to herself. That's just the shanachie, getting her tale straight."

I wonder what the workshop participants will think if I lie down at the front of the room and put the slide projector on my chest (not having a convenient rock) and start trying to get my tale straight. Women rattle their journals as they finish the writing exercise I gave them a few moments ago. I gather my notes and get ready to speak on the subject I love most, mindful listening. I say as I pace the front of the room, "Balance begins by going within and asking yourself first, 'What do I think? What do I feel? What do I need?' and then looking outside of yourself and seeing what others think, feel, and need. You get out of balance because you aren't listening to your inner life, because you aren't meeting the challenges of your life with any input from the inside. You haven't given yourself enough time to know what you think and feel."

As the words leave my mouth, it occurs to me that it has been months since I myself used mindful listening. Months? I can't remember the last time I stopped and checked in with myself. My heart sinks at the realization that this is yet another spiritual discipline I didn't stick with, and to make matters worse, a discipline of my own creation. I want to crawl under the lectern. I gaze at the questions beaming from the slide projector. The sound of the projector's fan rings in my ears as I read, "What one thing do I need most in the days ahead?" A voice says, "To listen." My attention snaps back to the audience. My heart thuds. Am I losing my mind? I've never had trouble keeping my attention focused when I'm speaking. I scan the room, hoping to spot the person who said "To listen," hoping I appear, if not brilliant, then at least sane. No one has her hand raised; no one waits expectantly for me to notice her.

I push the button on the slide projector and continue, all the while asking myself if that *very* loud voice was in my *head.*

Usually, after I speak, I "hermitize." I order room service, watch a movie, and tune out. It is my ritual. Tonight I am restless, jumpy. I can't stay in the hotel. I stroll along the square of this bustling New England college town, watching the students arriving for the fall semester, buying posters for their rooms, greeting each other over lattes, hanging out on the steps of the library. As I walk, I alternate between being angry at myself for forgetting to practice my own ideas and dismayed that when I ask, "What one thing do I need in the days ahead?" all I hear is a rushing babble. I need too many things: inner quiet, to write again, money, to feel confident as a mother, to be enraptured by, or at least tolerant of, my husband.

I head into a bookstore, thinking that perhaps an hour of browsing is the comfort I need. Perhaps I'll sit in the café and write my gratitude list. Oprah would approve.

I start in the children's section, looking for a birthday present for one of my daughter's friends. As I hold a copy of *The Stinky Cheese Man,* the title of Sue Monk Kidd's book *When the Heart Waits* squirms into my head. I had received this book years before but had given it away without reading it because it was "too Christian" for me. There doesn't seem to be a logical connection between *Stinky Cheese* and her book. I shrug and head for the religion section. It just seems to be a day for dictatorial inner voices. I find a lone copy of Kidd's book. I open randomly to the section entitled Live the Questions. I read, "One way we coax the life of the new self is by living the questions that inhabit our dark night, by dwelling creatively with the unresolved inside us." A page later, "There is an art to living your questions. You peel them. You listen to them. You let them spawn new questions. You hold the unknowing inside." A few paragraphs later, "The tension of the question itself seemed to bend and reshape me, drawing awareness into my path."

I sink down to the floor, holding the book gingerly. Goose bumps dot my arms and legs.

Questions. Listening. A theme emerges?

Later, when I have settled into bed and burrowed under the covers, I lie in the darkness, listening to a torrential spring rain pounding the hotel. What would it be like to hold the unknowing inside? I wonder. What would it be like to just sit with my mudflat of a life?

I lie very still, trying to let my grasping nature go, trying to accept the unknowing of my life, the disappointment I feel as, day after day, I watch the cool promise of the morning disappear into rushing, worrying, or doing inconsequential things. It occurs to me that even *trying* to accept it is too much action, too much doing. I try to stop that too. Finally, discouraged, I stop.

For one breath, I am inside the question, "What one thing do I need most in the days ahead?" For one breath, it doesn't matter that I don't have a clue.

Meeting the
Comfort Queen

After I returned home, I started asking myself, "What one thing do I need most?" I get up early, before my husband, Chris, and my daughter, Lilly, and plunk myself down on the couch and try to listen. Some mornings I inhabit that same place of not knowing I had felt in my hotel room, actually rest there for seconds at a time. That feels divine. Some mornings I bounce up after two minutes, too anxious and fearful to sit still—I don't want to know what is going on inside me. But bit by bit, I begin to hear modest, subtle prompts, like "Let go of your anger at Chris" and "Get some writing done before Lilly wakes up." Yet this makes it sound too concrete; it is often more of a feeling, like a gentle hand patting the small of my back.

Then one fall morning, as I waver between my desire to get up and my desire to let go, I hear, "Why not go somewhere and write? Why not take a retreat?"

I have to laugh out loud, which wakes my daughter. How many times had I fervently told women, "When you find yourself declaring that absolutely, no way, can you possibly take time off, that is *exactly* when you need to."

I also have to laugh at how obvious the solution was. The lid of a box I had been shut up in for months suddenly flew off. I stood up and looked around. Oh, yes, I could take a few days for myself and concentrate on what I wanted to write, what I wanted to do with my life. That was possible.

Of course, my critic began to yammer away at me almost at once. "You have no money. Where are you going to go on such short notice? Why don't you wait and go later?" The more he yammered, the more I knew I had to go, and go soon.

❀   ❀   ❀

It's two weeks later, and I am sitting in Marcie Telander's tiny tin-roofed cabin in the Colorado Rockies. I had first met Marcie—therapist, storyteller, ritualist, crone—on a canoe trip in New Mexico almost ten years before, when I was splayed out at another lost and desperate juncture. She spoke a nourishing language I had never encountered before, a language of self-acceptance and self-celebration that allowed me to be kind to myself on a much deeper level than I had ever thought possible. Years later, when a friend asked me when I had become a woman, I thought of that week on the Rio Chama.

Marcie's guest cabin was built in the 1920s and is filled to bursting with, among other things, two old iron bunkhouse beds, a potbelly stove, one perfectly preserved owl wing, a Navajo loom and rug, fur from the local white buffalo, childhood books from four generations of Telanders, about fifty pictures of beloved horses, and a pot to pee in.

I sit at the table in the center of this collection, attempting to write about being stuck. I have written fifty pages. Most of which isn't working. I'm Dorothy in the poppies. All I want to do is give in to the altitude and my fear of never writing another book and go to sleep.

Outside my open door the hazy sunshine glints off the hoods of the cars parked across the road. I pierce the dusty air with my voice: "Look, you came here to decide what to write. You are taking time away from your family. You have spent money to come here. This is a *writing* retreat. Get to work."

Write or sleep? Give up or buckle down? I'm skewed between indecision and self-loathing. Dopey, I stand up, fumble for my notebook and pen, and head for the creek, where Marcie keeps a student's desk tucked in among the willows. I move my pen in an effort to do what writers Natalie Goldberg, Julia Cameron, and other creativity gurus preach: get your pen moving, the great unknown will fill you up, be a faithful scribe. Show up and the

Divine will do the rest. How I detest this advice, I seethe, detesting it simply because I don't want to listen. I write what appears to be a laundry list of why I'll never write again.

I feel an abrupt breeze on my neck and a distinct tart mixture of clean sweat, fresh-cut grass, and what—it occurs to me later—must be hot chocolate chip cookies envelops me. I dutifully record this, keeping my pen moving. The breeze becomes more insistent, tugging at the pages of my journal. I slouch over, holding the journal open with my other hand and my elbow.

"Give it up, girl. It is time to stop writing and start leaping."

I jerk around and find myself staring at a six-foot-tall woman. She appears to be wearing a jeweled crown, the kind that makes you wonder how her neck can possibly support the weight, and the most resplendent pajamas I have ever seen, pajamas that shimmer with tea and toast and rainy days under quilts. Her cape is made of rose petals. The noonday sun is reflecting off a watering can into her face, so I can't quite make out her features.

"Who are you?" I say. My voice emerges as a tentative squeak.

She waves her hand as if to dismiss my question, and I hear small bells tinkle. "Here you are again, sinking into your own despair. When are you going to relax the grip, pry your fingers off the stick shift? You get your body to this divine place, but you leave your soul chained up in the basement, cleaning toilets. What am I going to do with you?"

She rustles past me, her cape whispering against my arm, and sprawls on the ground. The river alder twigs beneath her release their wine-dark musk, which mixes with her distinctive aroma. I still can't see her face clearly.

"Darling, I'm here to ask you, do you have the wherewithal, the courage, the stamina, to do what needs to be done? Do you have the trust, the love, the juicy juju, to stop? Take in the sail. Bring down the curtain. Whoa."

I want to tell her she is contradicting herself, but her words are melting around me like honey, gluing me into place.

"Who taught you not to trust yourself? Who taught you not to love yourself? It doesn't matter anymore. Because I'm here to teach you the Golden Rule of the Comfort Queen, the sutra of your muse. You teach everybody else. Who teaches the teacher? Every woman is a teacher, every woman needs to be taught, to be held. The first thing you've got to do is stop being so mental." She cackles at her own silly joke. I hear the distinct sound of a lighter being flicked and ice cubes dropping into a glass. Is she smoking a cigarette? Making a cocktail?

"The question to ask yourself is, How do you behave in a way that keeps food on the table and clean sheets on the beds *and* that keeps you connected, sweet girl, *connected* to the big energy source? With your attitude, you are *not* going to find the answer. No, ma'am. You aren't creating a life, you're mangling the one you've been given."

I am stung by her remarks and open my mouth to retort when her cool, slightly rough hands start rubbing the back of my neck, pressing my head down onto the desk, into a child's napping pose. She whispers in my ear: "I know my remarks hurt, but sometimes it takes a dose of what ails you before you can get well. Homeopathy of the spirit. What do you do when faced with the truth? You condemn yourself to death row, sleep on a bed of nails, tear at your hair, gnash your teeth. I'm here to help you face all that is slimy in you, but with compassion—compassion with a capital C, sweetheart. What you face with love makes you strong."

She leans over me as she speaks. "Whoever told you not to cry?"

"Who are you?" I mumble into my forearm, wondering how she knows I'm fighting back tears.

"I'm your Comfort Queen, honey, the muse come alive to love you and wake you *up.*"

I smell cigarette smoke. I sit up and blink at her. She is much shorter now, the same glinting light obscuring her face. She moves to one side, and I see it is not my preternatural visitor but Marcie. "Jennifer, I'm going for a hike before it rains. Do you want to come?" Marcie asks.

Disoriented, I wipe away my tears. "Marcie, I think I've been dreaming."

Marcie sits down on the ground and wraps her arms around her legs. "I'm listening."

A Few Brief Directions

NO ONE WAY

I wrote this book for all of us who eagerly cruise the stationery store aisles each December, licking our lips as we devour with our gaze the rows of shiny new day planners, ripe with promise. For those of us who attend outrageously expensive productivity seminars (with outrageously complicated organizers included), hoping to, once and for all, get our lives together. I wrote this book when I realized that the modern-day chimera, balance, is never coming home to roost *until* we stop looking for her outside of ourselves and start creating it from our essence.

In my own search, I discovered that balance is an inside job. I will never experience a week in which I give enough time and love to my daughter, the perfect amount of energy to my work, to my partnership, my friendships, my body, my spiritual life. That's a magazine article, not a life. What *is* possible? By slowing down and going inside to listen, by asking ourselves thought-provoking and specific questions, we can create wholeness and a certain kind of balance—realistic, unique to each of us, balance that is much more about connecting with the Divine than about a perfect schedule. We can take the old-time management maxim, "Do the most important thing first," to an entirely new level. By listening to the multitude of voices and experiences within us, as well as to our X chromosomes, to our instinct and reason, and to all the mysterious guidance available, we can sense, just there on the periphery, what our life story is about and what our next step must be. Because another fact has become abundantly clear to me and to the many women I interviewed: we can plan our lives, we can set goals, and that's useful and lovely, but we rarely end up where we think we will—and that's even lovelier; at least it will be lovelier if we can listen, trust, and surrender to where our life wants to lead us.

To create this kind of balance—what I call divine balance—you will need to experiment with the Living the Questions pages. These appear at regular intervals throughout this book—forty-two pages of questions in all. They comprise a spiritual life planner, a system of divine time management, the method by which you can make the inner life your daily bread. They will help you to integrate Buddhist monk Thich Nhat Hanh's guidance, "To love means to listen. Listening is a very important practice. There is a voice calling us and it wants us to listen. It may be that our body is calling us and wants us to listen to our body. It may be our feelings that are calling us and want us to listen to them. It may be our perceptions are calling us and want us to listen. It is very important for us to pay attention to the voice. The capacity of listening to ourselves is the foundation of the capacity of listening to others. The capacity to love others depends on the capacity of loving ourselves."

To best use the Living the Questions pages, it will help if . . .

You really, truly understand that there is no right way to do this. These questions are not meant to be another "should" on your to-do list. This is not about life-sweeping changes, mission statements, or finally getting it all together.

This is about modestly listening and following the guidance you receive, therefore . . .

Work at your own pace and above all, trust that pace.

Regular organizers batter you with guilt if you don't use each convoluted section twice a day. No stray slips of paper allowed. Keep everything neat in your binder under penalty of arrest by the organizational police. Here, on the other hand, we encourage sloth. We like slackers. We have bribed the organizational police on more than one occasion. Try this:

✸ **WRITE WHEN YOU NEED TO.** Reflect on a page of questions every week or so, writing and even sketching your reflections in a journal or ask yourself a question or two when you first awaken each morning. You can make these questions a part of other spiritual practices you may be exploring. Perhaps writing is not your thing. Fine. On your morning commute, instead of reading the paper or listening to the news, ask yourself a page of questions, ponder them in your heart. If an entire page of questions is overwhelming, then choose only one or two question to work with, the ones that furrow your brow with concentration, sink you into your fertile center. You can also walk the questions, dance them, draw them, sculpt them, sing them. Or maybe you prefer to take the questions into your meditation, yoga, or prayer practice? There is no right way to do it. Although it will help if you . . .

✸ **DON'T TRY TO DO THE QUESTIONS ALL IN ONE SITTING.** You could spontaneously combust. These question pages are meant to be used a little at a time, every few days or weeks. Time is your partner and ally here—the questions need time to ripen and work their magic. Imagine taking six months to a year to explore all the Living the Question pages. Read a few pages of the book, respond to a page of questions, and then let the whole shebang sit for a few days, a week, or however long *you* want. Or read the whole book and go back to the question pages. You will probably find it helpful to . . .

✸ **ESTABLISH A REGULAR LISTENING HABIT.** You could contemplate the questions:
  ✸ Early in the morning before work or before your family wakes up
  ✸ In the car while waiting for kids or your car pool
  ✸ In bed on Sunday night
  ✸ On your lunch hour on Monday
  ✸ With your women's group or book group
  ✸ Before your weekly lunch or dinner date
  ✸ After exercise

✸ **EXPERIMENT WITH GETTING OUT OF YOUR HEAD AND CRACKING YOUR HEART OPEN** before you encounter a page of questions. I have found that engaging my body allows me to listen more easily to where the questions want to take me. Doing three yoga sun salutations, breathing deeply and imagining divine love flooding me with each inhalation, stepping outside and observing the sky for a minute, walking around the block, reading the spiritual poetry of Rumi, Mary Oliver, Kabir—these will help you shift into listening mode. Astrologer Caroline Casey recommends imagining a line running down your spine and another line through your belly button, and putting your attention at the place where these two lines intersect. There you find your center, "the place of no fear."

My friend Kim shifts into listening mode by listening to spiritual books and lectures on tape as she drives around town doing her errands. Diane gets into the bathtub, often at 3:00 A.M. "when I can't sleep because I haven't been listening." Marcie finds speaking to herself kindly is imperative: "Listening requires a releasing of any overarching emotions. I have to talk myself into the pause that allows me to listen. First, how do I address myself? Am I spurring myself on, slave-driving myself? How am I blocking that still, quiet voice of wise support? On the simplest level, calling myself, 'You idiot!' or 'You fool!' blocks listening. It requires purposefully thinking of a love-name that has deep meaning for me. Regardless of what I am going to say to myself, I ask myself to preface it with 'My dear' or 'My dearest.' Then there's a pause where reflection has a bit of room to grow. The next thing I say to myself is 'It's okay. No matter what it is, it's okay. It's all right. I'm here.' That's an invitation to listen to the universal and the unique. Without an invitation, I think the inner council just screams. Every voice, every facet of the self we would like to harness for self-reflection, remains basically hysterical without a gentle, merciful invitation."

If you like, starting right now, you can begin a perpetual letter to yourself, creating a heart habit of unlimited richness and depth, a reflecting pond of all that is inside you.

Slide your hand over the cool page.

Why not leave the harried, exhausted, frazzled, and parched you behind? Or the you that knows everything because you've been doing inner work for so long? Or the you that knows nothing and prefers to eat crumbs rather than feast?

One antidote for stress and imbalance is listening to your deepest self before and during the craziness.

Another antidote is letting go of perfection.

There is no right way to do this. These words can be very potent if you take them in, if you really let yourself believe there is no right way. I'll never forget a retreat I led in which sweet Harriet, sitting next to me, on the fourth day of a five-day retreat, suddenly turned to me out of the blue and said, "There is no right way." She had such a look of amazement on her face. It was gorgeous to behold.

Climb into bed or up on the roof or run a bath or swing on the porch swing or find a quiet place in nature.

Take yourself by the hand. Experiment in the spirit of self-kindness.

WHAT IS THE ONE THING I NEED MORE OF IN MY LIFE RIGHT NOW?

Silence

Energy

Health

Rest

Time with my partner or
   close friend

Time with my children

Time alone

Creativity

Spiritual succor

Healthy food

Fresh air

Moving my body

Peaceful work environ-
   ment

Relaxed daily routine

Money

Fill in the blank: ____

Pick the one thing you need most. They may all feel necessary. When we are beginning this process, we can feel like great yawning holes of need. When I first started asking myself, "What do I need most right now?" I wrote, "I need to feel better, I need my head to be clear, I need to work, I need money, I need to not be so irritable all the time, I need to do something about my marriage, I need to spend more time playing with Lilly, I need to feel better . . ." I felt sucked under by my own needs. The Rice Krispy bars I had bought from the grocery called my name. "Come eat us and everything will be fine," they whispered. Instead of lunging for the kitchen, I stopped, took a deep, slow breath, and said a prayer, an act that startled me. "God, what can I do? I'm choking here. Give me some guidance." I sat, waiting. I didn't hear angels on high, but I did hear my inner voice say, quietly, calmly, "Choose one thing. Choose health."

I wonder if it is true, as some mystics and sages have said, that guidance is always available.

WHAT ONE MODEST STEP AM I WILLING TO TAKE TO GET MORE _____ IN MY LIFE?

Often, the first step is deciding if you really need it or if there is something else you would rather have. Second, allowing yourself to believe you *can* have it. For *modest* steps around my health, I wrote: "Take Saint-John's-wort, avoid wheat, listen to imagery tape before bed, take vitamins every day."

WHAT DO I NEED LESS OF IN MY LIFE?

Fear	Overdoing for others	Volunteer activities
Worry	Food	Junk or work reading
Work	Anxiety	E-mail
Anger	Clutter	Telephone messages
Noise	TV	Or _____

WHAT *ONE, MODEST STEP* AM I WILLING TO TAKE TO DECREASE ONE OF THESE THINGS IN MY LIFE?

Again, keep it small and don't commit to anything, no matter how small, unless you mean it. Make a not-to-do list with only one item. One small, doable something you can easily let go of.

That's all for now. Let this sit for a few days.

The Nudge We Need to Create Our Lives

My Comfort Queen, or CQ, as I've decided to call her, feels like a cross between Kitty from the TV show *Gunsmoke* and a West African Yoruba priestess, with a bit of Mother Mary thrown in. The Jungian contingent would no doubt call her my numinous inner guide, the Greeks my muse, the shamanic crowd my spirit guide. As for me, I've been wanting someone to run my life for years. I've decided to think of her as a feminine Jeeves the butler, arrived to bring some order to my existence.

It's later in the day. Outside my cabin the sky is bruised by an approaching thunderstorm, and the air is chilly. CQ and I lounge opposite each other on Marcie's pillow-strewn bed. Without preamble, CQ launches in: "The problem you and millions of other women are having is in some ways very simple. Don't think I'm politically naive. I'm a card-carrying member of NOW. I'm not denying that the system in place doesn't work for women or, for that matter, for anyone with a conscience and a care for the earth. But at our annual Comfort Queen convention, where all women's inner muses gather to compare notes, we realized you gals keep forgetting that you have the power to change some things. You definitely forget you have the power to change your attitude. Too often you're cramped in a narrow cage of your own making. You're trying to get free, but because you keep forgetting you are a pipeline for the creative juju of the Divine, you stay stuck. You and everyone else have the ability to make new out of old, a silk purse from a sow's ear, stone soup. You are bursting with life, and yet the same attitudes and beliefs keep tripping you up. I decided you needed a helpful nudge."

She sees my skeptical expression and pats my leg. "You aren't seeing that life is a creative act. Because your work is creative you believe your life is creative and has enough meaning. A typical mistake. The truth is, it's not what you do, it's how you do it." CQ looks around the cabin. "They've got everything in here but a soapbox. I like a good soapbox."

CQ is half hidden in the shadows and from where I'm sitting, she appears gauzy, insubstantial. She is, it seems, fading in and out.

"You always have a choice, Jennifer. You can accept that guidance is available at all times, or you can do what you've been doing for the last two years—or, come to think of it, it's been quite a bit longer than that—and turn away. Believe me: guidance is always available. It is around you, in you, and quite literally bombarding you. You have to get still enough, respectful enough, to hear it. As the great fourteenth-century mystic Julian of Norwich said, 'All shall be well, and all manner of things shall be well.' But only if you have faith that they will be." On the word "faith," CQ rumbles her voice like a revival-style preacher.

She has my full attention now. Her outline fills in and her crown fills the dim cabin with a lustrous heat. "I'm listening." When I say that, a key clicks softly somewhere in a hidden keyhole. "I'm listening," I say again, just for the pleasure of hearing it.

"Every woman and every man is given a unique set of treasures to create with. You've got to *see* those treasures." CQ produces a cigar box. "You've got to protect these treasures. You've got to create with what you've been given rather than obsess about what you wish you'd been given." She opens the cigar box and holds it under the reading lamp. Jumbled words are inside, jumping and jostling one another like eager puppies. Out of this quivering, upside-down mosaic, I make out some words: *tenacious, well-developed sense of the absurd, loyal, enterprising, clear-sighted.* Then CQ shuts the box with a snap.

"I hear everybody yammering on about balance and not enough time. But I don't see anybody realizing that you create your life from the inside out. Everything starts inside—the inside has to shape the outside, not the other way around. Here you are, running from car pool to work to your women's group, letting that outer stuff whittle the shape of your life. You are letting what others think of you, want from you, or what you think they must have from you, do the same. You've got to go inside, listen, and ask, 'How does my inner life want to shape my outer life?' That's the discipline. That's the key that so many of you aren't practicing."

Guilt and doubt wash over me, causing CQ to flicker and grow dim. She's reading my mind. No, she's *in* my mind. "You are thinking, 'Like that's friggin' possible when Lilly is having a temper tantrum, the house is a mess, Chris is out of town, and I'm on deadline. Get real.' Here's the truly amazing part you have got to embrace: it is possible; it really is."

I write down what she says, but I've retreated to that place inside me where all I can think about is shutting down, having a glass of wine, anything but thinking about these colossally daunting notions. CQ's voice is faint as she says, "Start by asking and listening. Start by living the questions. Rilke was onto something when he said that the point is to live everything. 'Live the questions now. Perhaps you will then gradually, without noticing it, live along some distant day into the answer.' Make this your daily practice. And be kind to yourself while you're at it."

"What questions am I trying to live?"

"I'll give you some to start with, a framework. Some you will have to go on a scavenger hunt for. Some will bubble up from deep within you as we explore your unfolding path together. Not to worry, the questions are there."

I look up from writing. CQ has vanished.

I slap my notebook shut and complain aloud, "I'm stuck in an episode of *Bewitched,* taking advice from Endora." I consider this for a moment. "I always did like Agnes Moorehead's character the best."

Endora was very good at taking care of herself.

Living the Questions

2

WHAT ARE MY MOST COMMON OBSTACLES TO RELAXATION AND SELF-NURTURING RIGHT NOW?

Not enough time   Guilt
Not enough money   Feels selfish
Children   Don't know where to start
Work   Feels too needy
Confusion

Name a few details about what blocks rest and renewal for you. Don't fill up a thousand pages, just list the top one hundred. Or ten. Or five. Or three. Throw in one belief or attitude for spice. Mine are my tense attitudes about work, worry about money, low energy, Chris traveling, being a mom.

HOW MANY OF THESE OBSTACLES DO I CHOOSE TO KEEP IN MY LIFE?

How can you grasp that creating your life is first a decision, a commitment? To begin this process of listening is to say, "Everything inside of me has value and I will listen to it." This requires courage—valuing our own hearts enough to heed them.

WHAT ARE THE SIGNS THAT I'M GETTING OUT OF HARMONY?

Complaining a lot   Garden neglected
Irritable as a baby with diaper rash   Almost having a car accident
Feel like you're walking through mud   Message machine so full it can't take
Jealous   any more messages
Too much solitude   Everything feels urgent
Overspending   Miss church, women's group, Sunday
Talking and moving fast   morning phone call to Mom
Back, head, neck, or stomach hurts

(continued on next page)

Living the Questions

continued

Be a detective of your life for a few days. Come back and record what you find, the unique signs that you are getting out of whack. This is *not* an invitation to self-judgment but a step on the path of awareness.

ARE ANY OF THOSE SIGNS HAPPENING NOW?
IS THERE ONE ACTION I COULD TAKE
TO BRING A BIT OF HARMONY AND RELIEF
TO ONE AREA OF MY LIFE?

Take note: a *bit* of harmony to *one* area. One tiny action in body, spirit, creative endeavors, family, attitude, work, sex life, home, love, community?

Breathe in self-kindness.
Breathe out judgment.

Let what you discovered percolate in you for the next few days.

Why Questions?

I'm sitting on the deck in the early morning silence, hands wrapped around my tea, pondering the questions.

But why questions? Author and professor Maria Harris reminds me that "The spiritual world is question based." In *Dance of the Spirit* she writes, "First we must reshape and redesign the undersong of our lives—the innerness of our lives—according to a form and a framework that allows us to live the questions, love the questions, dance the questions. And second, we must pause, rest, and reflect, allowing ourselves the unhurried time brought by silence, prayer, and contemplation in order to help our spirituality flourish." Domenica Bianca, who does energy healing and is a modern-day mystic, said, "The presence of a question mark is the presence of God. Where black-and-white is present, God usually isn't." When we ask ourselves questions, we turn within and access our desires, our opinions. In time, "genuine listening gives birth to genuine hearing." When we begin to hear, we also begin to ask, Why is this so? Why did this happen? Who decided it would be that way?

I had been searching for years for a way to organize my life: visualizing my heart's desire, writing crisp sheets of goals, faithfully following Stephen Covey's bustling *Seven Steps for Highly Effective People* organizer, even inventing systems of my own. Yet they all failed because they imposed an outside shape on my life. I was left trying to squeeze myself into that shape instead of naturally growing into my own distinct curves. In 1926, in *A Life of One's Own,* Marion Milner wrote about her attempts to discern what made her happy: "I had been continually exhorted to define my purpose in life but I was now beginning to doubt whether life might not be too complex a thing to be kept within the bounds of a single formulated purpose, whether it would not burst its way out or, if the purpose was too strong, perhaps grow distorted like an oak whose trunk has been encircled with an iron band. . . . *So I began to have an idea of my life, not as a slow shaping of achievement to fit my preconceived purposes, but as the gradual discovery and growth of a purpose which I did not know.*"

I had been trying to fit my life into a preconceived form. There was another way, and it had been attempting to get my attention for years: my own avid interest in questions and the system of check-in I had been teaching. Yet I had never applied the idea to my life in a consistent and progressive way. I had been looking for the thread of my life outside myself, hoping to find an answer to my confusion in some prescription.

"You are treading on dangerous ground. You start a new project, and you decide it's the best thing since sliced bread. You're going to get all riled up about these questions, and you'll burn out. You have not discovered the Holy Grail." I look down at my journal, from where the voice is emanating. There, animatedly wriggling on the page, her body curved into the form of a question mark wearing a miniature crown, is CQ. She wags her finger at me. "You've got to take this slowly."

I take a sip of my tea and notice my hand is shaking. Twenty years ago I would have thought a hallucination of this magnitude was one wicked acid flashback. Now I wonder if it's too much yoga and gingko biloba.

"Here's the thing," CQ says as she bounces across my journal, turning the pages until she finds a blank one. "You have the choice to build your life around inner direction or on the external, eternal whine, 'Look how much I have to do.' The Divine Intelligence doesn't care how much you have to do. She cares that you are paying attention."

"Okay." I try to breathe deeply. "I'm paying attention. You started off by saying I was on dangerous ground."

CQ flips open the period that punctuates the bottom of her question mark. A pen nib emerges. She grins. "I love thingamajigs. Remind me to show you my satellite-phone wristwatch." She twirls across the page, drawing spirals in Day-Glo orange ink.

"Here, I'll make you a list. I know how you love lists." She writes:

✴ **TAKE YOUR TIME.** Take it slow. When you get overwhelmed, stop.

CQ the pen looks up at me, checking to see that I follow. I nod. She draws a large spiral across the page, then writes, "Life interrupts."

✴ **LIFE IS SUPPOSED TO INTERRUPT.** Don't expect it to be any different.

CQ fixes her gaze on me: "You are not going to use the questions every day. Do not cook up a fantasy of a new, improved you. You've got to toss out your expectations of perfection about working with me and with these questions. Or continue to be burdened with them. It is your choice. But I'm here to make at least one point crystal clear: Life doesn't get resolved. Resistance, interruptions, and fear are as valid as understanding, flow, and joy. There isn't any difference. It is all a continuum."

My stomach is fluttering. I realize I'm feeling both excited and frightened by her words. "Life never gets resolved. . . . It sounds so grim."

CQ is getting carried away, covering every page with spirals. "We'll talk more about that later. For now, just remind Mr. Critical that this book may not be used as a bludgeon. Remind him that there is no right way." CQ adds to her list.

✴ **MAKE FRIENDS WITH MS. RESISTANCE.** I can hear her knocking on the door right now. Ask her in for a snack. Instead of hating her, see what she has to say. Same with old habits, deadlines, other people's emergencies. They will all take over your life at some point and you will forget to work with these questions I'm giving you. So what?

The way of creating my life that CQ is describing is somewhat different from my usual, shall we say, rather controlling approach. I take a slow, deep breath. CQ keeps writing.

✴ **SELF-NURTURING DISCIPLINE.**

"Discipline. That word makes my skin break out," I complain.

"Here's a paradox, the first of many we'll encounter. Give yourself a break, go at your own pace, *and* be disciplined. Your idea of discipline is based on fear and self-distrust. The discipline it takes to live the questions is *never* based on self-hatred or fear. I'm going to teach you how to walk the tightrope between the desire to know yourself and the pull of being unconscious but agreeably numb.

With me at your side, you'll see how to curb your tendency to overdo it or hide or be hard on yourself."

"So what you're saying," I venture, "is take it slow and don't go overboard. Delve at my own pace. Let resistance seduce me into giving up, and yet love myself enough to stick with the whole process?"

CQ pirouettes from question mark pen into full Comfort Queen form, grabs my hands, spins me around the deck. "That's exactly it."

The trees spin with me.

Living the Questions

3

AS I BREATHE AND VISUALIZE THE COMING MONTH OR SO,
WHAT ARE THE TWO OR THREE PLACES IN MY LIFE WHERE I FEEL
THE MOST STRESS? WHAT TIES ME IN KNOTS, MAKES ME
LOSE MY TEMPER OR CHAFE WITH IRRITATION?

Choose something specific. Instead of saying, "I don't have enough money to pay the bills," name the bills you can't pay. Instead of saying, "Julie, the woman who co-owns the yoga studio with me," write, "When Julie reschedules classes without telling me."

STRESS POINTS AND DISCOMFORTS

No fixing, no action, simply cataloging.

(continued on next page)

HOW CAN I NURTURE MYSELF IN THE DAYS AHEAD?

Hints:

PLAYFUL INTERLUDE: Groucho glasses, henna tattoos, squirt bottles, watermelon seed–spitting contest, e-mail jokes saved to read when in need of a laugh . . .

EMOTIONAL HEALING: Writing about an upsetting event, working at a soup kitchen, starting therapy, ending therapy, taking a shower and imagining the pain washing away . . .

BODY RELAXATION: A peppermint foot bath, taking a thermos of herbal tea to work, lavender eye pillows, sugar-free Popsicle, sauna or steam bath, new vibrator, Brazilian dance class, flow yoga video . . .

HOW HAVE I BEEN TALKING TO MYSELF LATELY?
AM I TALKING TO MYSELF LIKE SOMEONE I LOVE?
IF NOT, COULD I CHOOSE TO SAY SOMETHING ELSE INSTEAD?
CQ NOTES: "BE A GEISHA TO YOURSELF."

Remember, there is no right way to do this. The focus is simply on listening.

Living First by What We Treasure

For the last few years, I have observed a growing number of women who know how to take care of themselves, who in varying degrees have emerged from years of therapy, from piles of self-help books, from retreats and ashrams, and are no longer seeking. They have reached a point—often after hitting the wall of exhaustion, failure, or tragedy—from which they can begin to accept themselves and their lives as they are. They have ridden the pendulum, swinging far to one side in an effort to grasp power and freedom. Now they are swinging back to the middle and, in doing so, creating a new way of being, a new way of creating their lives, a genuine form of power. These are not perfectly realized, enlightened goddesses but rather women who had, as writer and editor Priscilla Stuckey put it, used their limitations, their disappointments, and their disasters "like keyholes through which we can peep and see no limitations."

"These women are finding ways to live their lives from the inside out." CQ materializes on top of my computer monitor. She is the size of a Barbie doll but much more voluptuous. Her petite legs dangle over my screen. "They probably have found their Comfort Queens, their inner nurturing muses, although each may name her something different. To rediscover the thread of your life, your unfolding path, you need to learn from these women, seek them out, connect with their knowledge."

"That sounds lovely, but what am I going to ask them?"

CQ opens her tiny eyes wide. "Observe your life. What are you struggling with? How are you creating your life? Or perhaps the question is, How are you *not* creating your life?"

That remark hurts. CQ shrugs. "Honey, I am not all sweetness and light. That was the New Age eighties. Thank God, that phase is over. I'm going to love you, and anyone else who cares to listen, into a better place, but I'm like a best friend, I speak the truth. That's the only way you stay real friends." She reaches out a tiny hand and pats my face. It reminds me of what Lilly used to do when she was a baby, and I sigh with joy. CQ pats me once more, then begins to shrink. As she shrinks, her voice gets louder instead of softer. "Your life is the guide." I stand up to see what's happened to her. On top of my monitor is a postage stamp with her profile on it. When I touch it, she winks at me and then disappears in a poof of shimmering dust.

I sit back down. Follow my life? Now, *that* didn't sound very promising. CQ's voice booms from everywhere and nowhere, "'Have you ever noticed that in order to hate yourself, you have to give yourself a lot of attention? A passing insult or an occasional barb won't do it. Self-abuse is a full-time occupation. It takes everything you've got in order to feel like nothing.' That's from Naomi Newman's play *Snake Talk*. Now stop playing small and get to work."

I speak to the ceiling, not sure where she is. "Easy for you to say. I don't see you sitting here trying to write."

"You writers are the most self-pitying and dramatic lot I've ever met. Remember, guidance and inspiration are always available. Don't go on your will alone, get some help. This time I'm really leaving." My study room door breezes shut with a playful slam.

Help. Get some help. What an tantalizing idea. A friend had been keeping company with three native medicine women. They told her, "Help is always available, but you have to ask." My friend replied, "I do ask, when I am in despair." One of the women shrugged, "If you just want to use the EMT version, go ahead."

That was me too, EMT all the way. I had been working with Domenica on my healing and she kept telling me the same thing: "As you sit down to write, before you go into what is a mental focus for you, consciously open to inspiration, allow yourself to be God-soaked and not to feel that is in any way different from when you actually focus yourself on the task, on the writing itself."

I sit at my desk, fingers in ears so I can hear the sound of my breath and only the sound of my breath, not Lilly playing in her room, not Chris on the phone, not the chain saw somewhere nearby. God-soaked. What is that? How do I do it? I want to do it right. Maybe I don't have to *do* anything, just ask and allow divine energy in. I watch worries flit across the screen of my mind, stomping on the guidance that is trying to spring up. How afraid I am. Why? Trust. "Trust," I repeat over and over. Trust your work.

Trust my work? Where did that notion come from? A quote came to mind, and I went in search of the exact words: "Until we prioritize our lives according to what's important to us individually, we will remain in need of the external reinforcement we get from our jobs. We are all too aware of what we sacrifice for work, but if we don't put those things on the agenda, work will always come first. . . . We can have it both ways. As long as we live first by what we treasure, and let the rest fall into place," Elizabeth Perle McKenna wrote in *When Work Doesn't Work Anymore.* I thought about the many women I had met who had transformed their work lives, created their own jobs, their own businesses, or found companies to work for where the treatment and hours were more humane, more "feminine." As much as I loved hearing that women were remaking work, I had never deeply related to their stories because I felt immune. Look at me, doing what I love, no boss. Financial stress, sure, but, hey, that's the trade-off.

But doing what I loved had sent me into the pit of despair.

Was I living first by what I treasured? The women I admired certainly were. They had found what they treasured while I resonated more with being "in need of external reinforcement."

"That's good." CQ appears as my screensaver, her pixilated face spinning. "That's a very good clue. Follow that thought!" A horse appears on the screen, CQ jumps on and gallops into infinity. I watch her disappear into my computer and wish I could follow her.

Because I don't want to follow this thought.

WHAT IS ONE THING I'M FEELING STRESS OR DISCOMFORT ABOUT?

Look back at what you named on page 23.

WHAT COULD THIS STRESS OR DISCOMFORT BE ASKING ME TO DEVELOP? HOW COULD IT BE HELPFUL OR BENEFICIAL TO MY LIFE'S DEVELOPMENT?

For example, stress for Judy was meeting with a number of important men in her field. When she questioned what this stress was asking her to develop, Judy wrote: "It's asking me to develop my business sense, to take myself seriously, to break through old beliefs. It could be beneficial because I might make contacts, and the more I put myself in these situations, the more I see whether this is what I want to do with my life or not."

WHOM COULD I ASK FOR ONE SMALL ACT OF SUPPORT OR FOR ONE SPLENDID IDEA TO EASE MY STRESS OR DISCOMFORT?

We are fabulous at helping others. We are terrible at asking for help. Ask directly, gently, without shame or guilt, and choose carefully whom you ask. I often sabotage myself by asking a friend for help who is also in crisis. Start small (another mantra). Ask Spirit or a help line, or e-mail an advice Website. The point is to remind ourselves, again and again, that we do not have to do this alone.

Breathing in, say silently to yourself, "I am not all things."
Breathing out, repeat, "And I am enough."

Louden Lane

In Indiana, where five generations of both sides of my family, including myself, were born, there is a road named after my family. The post at the beginning of this very short road displays three signs. They read, Dead End, No Outlet, Louden Lane. In that order.

The Dead End and No Outlet signs are considerably larger than the Louden Lane sign.

Beginning in adolescence, along with the rest of the world, I felt inferior. I was a skinny thing with bad skin and a permanent sunburn from basking my Scotch-Irish skin in the sunshine of Florida, where we moved when I was two. A walking bundle of wired energy with not enough outlets to siphon it off, I spent a tremendous amount of my time worrying about what others thought of me and being boy-crazy. None of this changed much in college, although my skin cleared up and I became chubby instead of skinny. I was always falling a little short of my best effort. Sometimes more than a little. I graduated from college and had the same experience in the work world and, later, in the screenwriting trade. I was smart enough to draw near to the brass ring, but every time I got close to grasping it, I became distracted with what someone else thought of me, and the prize slipped through my fingers.

At around twenty-five, a few years after finishing film school and embarking on a screenwriting career, I started listening to what was going on inside me, not for the first time, but this time I was in enough pain to heed what I was hearing. It was as if I had given up a five-cup-a-day Starbucks habit and I could sit still long enough to hear the voice inside, a voice that turned out to be neither still nor small in its insistent demand that I quit writing. Yet I literally felt I would die if I quit. I had no idea how to exist without moving ahead with some grand project, some life-changing scheme. "Choose emptiness? Open myself to the possibility of becoming something else? No way!" was my refrain. It took tremendous pain to push me into such a tight corner that I had to listen. That corner consisted of being unable to walk for three months because of a skiing accident, then wrecking my car so I couldn't go anywhere, and joy! Best of all, writer's block. I had no choice but to take what I called a month or two off. When I actually accepted this, without making bargains in my head or secretly hoping for something different, there was a tremendous feeling of relief and in that pure moment, the title for my first book, *The Woman's Comfort Book,* an exploration of how to be kind to yourself, popped into my head as clear as if you said it now.

I had given up willing my life to happen the way I wanted it to. I had dared to let go of self-imposed ambitions. I had committed my first genuinely self-nurturing act, my first leap of faith. "Be open to the meaning in what you did not want to happen," writes Robert Hopcke in his book on synchronicity *There Are No Accidents.* He goes on to say we need "an attitude of openness, an ability to set aside our own agendas" so that we can "allow the meaning of what seems initially like mere bad luck to flower into what it is destined to be." I would add that we also need a tractor-trailer load of patience and courage.

Of course, I had no idea about any of this at the time, nor did I go willingly. Even now, when I look back, I think, Wasn't there an easier way? Nope. The part of me who knew what I most needed to do had decided I was going to write self-help books.

This self, however, neglected to tell me exactly what the title meant. I continued writing lame stories in an attempt to be a screenwriter (my desire to do what I wanted had asserted itself after a few months, and I started writing again even though I was terribly unhappy—this kind of amnesia is part of the process), all the while being beguiled and pestered by this title that would not go away. Slowly and in exceedingly circuitous ways, I began to explore writing a book about women's comforts.

Remain alert to the next prompting!

When the book was published, I got what I had always wanted: to feel okay about myself because someone else valued my work. I got to feel "an expanded sense of personal importance, choice, mastery, and psychic empire building" as Naomi Wolf describes it in *Fire with Fire.* That part was great. I developed faith in myself, a healthy feeling of confidence. The part that made me stumble and plunge into the pit was that I began, subtly and without conscious awareness, to focus on the outside reaction, the result, what other people thought of me, to equate myself with my work. Instead of remaining alert to the next prompting (in creative terms, lying fallow and waiting for inspiration; in feminist language, being self-referenced; in Western religious terms, surrendering to God's will, and in Eastern philosophical language, watching for the unfolding path), I trained my eye on external stuff. I wanted to keep up with and add to my newly acquired sense of self-worth. Becoming a successful writer had allowed me to transcend the feeling that I wasn't okay. So of course when I stopped feeling successful—when my book sales slowed, when my writing went on walkabout again, and when I suffered a terrible case of professional jealousy that had nothing to do with talent and everything to do with another writer's net worth—the feeling of not being good enough returned. With a vengeance.

My wounded ego was soothed a bit when I asked teacher, astrologer, and therapist Jennifer Freed about women who had found themselves in similar situations. "I see women trying to find the Muse within," she said. "It means very different things for different women. Some women always wished they had danced and never did and now they are forty. Oh, well, they think. But then they start taking dance classes and it is something they commit to. It's not about becoming the best dancer. Because that is over with. All these activities from the very get-go are not about becoming famous or well-loved or recognized. Women are returning to things they abandoned in pursuit of just that. It didn't get them love, and so now they are doing them out of love. And that's a very different turn. They've stopped trading in their heart's desire for something they think will be marketable."

Here's how tricky this whole business of creating a life is: I never thought I was trading in my heart's desire; I thought I was following it.

Living the Questions

5

WHAT ONE THING COULD I DO IN THE DAYS AHEAD TO BECOME THE PERSON I MOST WANT TO BE?

Think small and be sure you *really* want to do what you write down. I wrote, "Participate in Lilly's school even though I'm shy." Why force myself to do this? Because part of who I want to become is someone who realistically and wholeheartedly lives in a community made up of all kinds of people, not only the ones I'm comfortable with.

WHERE OR WHEN DO I FIND MYSELF FOCUSING OUTSIDE OF MYSELF?

When I started to examine this tendency, I found I did this a lot, like a sort of built-in comparison shopper. Corporate trainer Jinny Ditzler makes a great point in her book *Your Best Year Yet.* Many of us, especially women, make this question the focus of our lives: What can I do to prove myself? By asking ourselves this, we reinforce the idea that we are intrinsically not good enough and we place our worth on the approval of others. Instead, we can ask, "What can I do with the gifts I have?" This puts us in a position of inner power, creating solutions, and focusing on our strengths. Try using the second question throughout your day to reframe feelings of inadequacy, the need for approval, or moments of feeling overwhelmed.

WHAT CAN I DO TODAY WITH THE GIFTS I HAVE?

HOW HAVE I BEEN TALKING TO MYSELF LATELY? LIKE SOMEONE I LOVE OR SOMEONE I LOATHE?

Check in with the radio station of your mind. What station is it on?

CQ reiterates, "If the questions start to feel like too much, put the book down, and feel me taking your arm. If you let me, I'll lead you to exactly what you need to do to relax and listen."

More Than Intuition

The stories I like about people creating their lives are tales of enormous risks taken, stable, cushy, even glamorous lives discarded. These people bet the farm, and win triumph in the form of a renewed vision and purpose, and often a decent bank account, too. They are the winners of the consciousness lottery. See what you get if you have faith, visualize, and follow your inner voice!

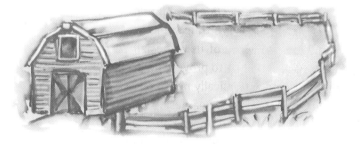

But these tales can be misleading because they can imply spiritual material-ism—"Listen and you will be amply rewarded"—and they can make the path of listening seem like a do-it-once-and-you're-set-for-life venture. But that isn't true. Oriah Mountain Dreamer, in her book *The Invitation,* frames the quest this way: "We are not offered guarantees. What we are offered is knowledge of life and ourselves, and if we are awake, glimpses of the wisdom held in the story our life is telling the world."

Divine balance is about *continually* listening to the story our life is telling the world. Saral is a nondenominational minister who learned to listen because, like many of us, she was desperate enough. She also learned to *keep* listening. "I learned to follow my inner voice," she said, "because I had no choice." Saral and I are tucked away in her hobbit cottage on a blustery winter afternoon, drinking decaf English Breakfast tea by the fire, fending off her husband's sweet, lick-crazy dog.

"My life was a life born into abuse," Saral told me. "It was a life of a lie. It was the happy family that hid a bunch of abuse, and I lived an unconscious life until I was in my thirties. I got married when I was eighteen. I did everything I was supposed to do. I started creating my life when I was twenty-four years old. I had a profound dream that I was in a cage and I had to get out. There was light outside of my cage. After that dream, I suffered through eight weeks of insomnia. The doctor was going to hospitalize me, and instead, I got divorced. I woke up one morning and said, 'I can't live with you anymore.' Divorcing him didn't make logical sense. He was a great friend to me. It wasn't a great marriage, but it wasn't anywhere near where I thought divorce was. He was my father's favorite student and he adored my father. I would never have remembered my childhood if I had not divorced him. That was the beginning of 'I have a knowing that is so insistent.' That was the beginning of creating my life.

"Several years later, I was hit with a wave of depression. My inner voice got loud enough for me to follow. I got in my car with no idea where I was going or how long I would be gone. I only knew I was in too much pain not to listen. I had a thousand dollars to my name. I thought I would end up farther north, but when I stopped in Ashland, Oregon, I knew it was the place. My time in Ashland gave me a freedom I had never known: I could cry whenever I wanted to, and that was the best gift. Right before I left Ashland, I spent a week in the woods alone. I have never felt safer or more connected to God.

"After these three incredible, painful months I drove back home, stopping in San Francisco to confront my father about how he had abused me. I spent the night before this with my sister, and everything I had taken to Ashland was stolen out of my car—my clothes, my journals, my books—everything that had meaning, so that when I drove to the therapist's office to meet with my father the next day, I had nothing with me. It was so odd and so right. I drove back home a new person. I began a life less encumbered by the past. In the years since, I have decided to live by that voice. Still, I am afraid of her because . . . look at the two things she has asked me to do. It can be hard to trust her. Yet I know it led me to the happiest times of my life. Now my life is a constant trying to listen. To ask, What do I need to do? What's my next step? It's all balanced with a curiosity, with hope."

Am I talking about listening to your intuition? Yes and no. Through my years of practicing and neglecting listening, and through my research, I have found that intuition is only one name for listening, and one that often is linked to predicting the future, which is handy, but what we're talking about here is much bigger than that. Then perhaps we're listening to the unconscious, as in Jung's definition of the unconscious: "Everything of which I know, but of which I am not at the moment thinking; everything of which I was once conscious but have now forgotten; everything perceived by my senses, but not noted by my conscious mind; everything which, involuntarily and without paying attention to it, I feel, think, remember, want, and do; all the future things that are taking shape in me and will sometime come to consciousness: all this is the content of the unconscious."

"That just about covers it, doesn't it? That man had an exceedingly thorough mind." I look up from my computer to see CQ lounging in the doorway.

"Can you help me?" Before the words are out of my mouth, I feel this incredible lightness surging throughout my being. CQ smiles.

"Magic words, aren't they—'Can you help me?' I'd be delighted. Here's how I see it. You are listening to God."

"We're venturing out of listening to ourselves and into God territory, are we?" I feel unease at the G-word but try not to show it.

CQ roars with laughter. "You have to be the most dualist person on the face of the earth. What makes you think your authentic self and God are any different? Or that one self is more authentic than any other? You'll soon get to a point where *names* don't matter. Call it Divine Intelligence, Big Mind—shoot, how about, Holy Soul, Jelly Roll, à la Allan Ginsberg? What you *think* you are listening to, conversing, or arguing with at any one time depends on your history, the pesky little genes everyone is so in love with these days, and a host of other particulars. What matters is not naming but *practice.* Showing up and being open to listening to all the voices and sources. Teasing out and having a dialogue with everything, engaging in a *lifelong* process of sorting your truth from the noise of the greedy world, the shame from your fifth grade math teacher, even the demands of your beloved family. The sources you are listening to bleed into each other, like watercolors. So you must learn to practice discernment."

I nod slowly. "Discernment. That reminds me of what theologian Mary Davies said. She worries that listening to yourself "can sometimes be a shallow place, a reflecting pool. Instead of seeing the depths of what's there, all you see is your face, which is not enough."

CQ goes to one of my perilously overstuffed bookcases and pulls out *Coming Home to Myself* by Marion Woodman. She opens the book and reads, " 'Don't talk about *being true to myself* until you are sure to what voice you are being true.' Marion and Mary are saying the same thing. Creating your life from the inside out means constantly appraising where you are getting your guidance from."

"So tell me how I'm supposed to practice discernment in this situation. In the last few days, I've been trying to make a business decision about whom to partner with on a project. When I listen, I'm pulled in one direction by pride; I want to go with the business partner who has the higher profile and the bigger booth at trade shows. Then another voice chimes in, the voice of my good girl who doesn't want to hurt anyone's feelings, doesn't want to choose one person over another. Finally there is this loud, lush, greedy voice that says, 'Go with the one who offers us the most. Let's make money and buy things!' It's been impossible to get past these voices to my authentic voice."

"Why is that a problem?" CQ starts to sit on the small wicker chair near my desk. She frowns at it and a huge fluffy purple chaise appears in its place. She makes herself comfortable, then continues. "When all your inner voices are considered instead of judged, they relax. Just like when you stop and *hear* your daughter, she relaxes. Your inner selves do the same. The ugly voices especially need your attention. You should see them. They sigh and lie back. 'Ah, I'm being perceived.' They aren't any more or less authentic. Listening to everyone at your inner party is a surefire way to clear away the smoke of confusion and get a glimpse of your unfolding path."

"Are you saying it doesn't matter who I'm listening to as long as I listen and don't judge what I hear?"

CQ pats the chaise and I leave my office chair to sit beside her. "What I'm saying," she says, "is surrender to your inner process instead of trying to label it. Jung said, 'What is not brought to consciousness comes to us as fate.' If you judge one voice as better than the other, or one desire as more appropriate, you are basically saying either 'I cannot trust myself' or 'I'm not really listening because this is what I plan on doing anyway,' and both cloud the picture. Listen by surrendering. And remember that listening doesn't mean you have to act on what you hear."

I examine CQ's crown rather than look into her penetrating eyes. "Surrender has always been a difficult concept for me," I say. "It seems so"—I think for a moment—"so passive."

CQ tickles my arm gently. "I know how hard this is for you. That's one of the reasons I'm here, to crack your rigid need to know. That more than anything gets in the way of listening. Surrender is anything but passive. You know how hard it is to float on your back, say, on a lake?"

I nod.

"Surrendering to this process is very similar. You have to make subtle adjustments to keep your legs up and your head back, and every now and then a little wave throws you off-balance. But through it all, you are being held up by the water. There is an effortlessness to it."

I tilt my head back, imagine floating on a mountain lake. A ripple of delight runs through me, quickly followed by helplessness and sheer vulnerability.

CQ pats my leg. "That's enough for today. When was the last time you swung like a child in the hammock in the backyard with Lilly and read together?"

I close my eyes and try to remember the last time Lilly and I lounged. When I open them to reply, CQ has vanished, and a pile of enticing children's books has taken her place.

Living the Questions

6

AM I DOING SOMETHING FOR SOMEONE ELSE
THAT I NEED TO BE DOING FOR MYSELF?

What do you need that you won't claim for yourself but are happily or not so happily giving to others?

WHAT AM I DOING FOR MYSELF THAT I COULD
BE DOING FOR SOMEONE I LOVE?

Be careful with this second question. It is not meant to induce guilt but to wake up women like me who are great at self-nurturing but not so good at nurturing others. This question alerted me to a hazardous imbalance with my partner. Because I was good at taking care of myself, I claimed more time for myself than he did. Also, because he felt guilty for traveling on business so much, he often did little for himself when home, even when months passed between his trips. To deal with this, I had to walk the line between caretaking—"Oh, you aren't good at this, I'll tell you what you need to do"—and being selfish. Here is an approach that seems to be helping: "Honey, I would like to go to yoga Saturday morning. If you'd like to do something for yourself this weekend, I'd be happy to take Lilly Sunday morning." Taking me up on that offer is his responsibility. Mine is being sure I'm not always grabbing everything for myself or subtly sending him signals to work more and play not at all. All that said, be careful with this second question—don't use it to induce great fits of chest-beating and hair-tearing.

IF THE MOST PROFOUND WAY TO RECEIVE GUIDANCE WERE TO SAY TO
THE DIVINE, "I AM READY TO LISTEN," WOULD I BE ABLE TO SAY THAT IN
THIS MOMENT? WHAT WOULD IT FEEL LIKE TO GET OUT OF MY OWN WAY?

CQ nudges you with her hip: "The way you get out of your own way is to stop trying to get out of your own way."

Living the Questions

continued

HOW CAN I ACT AS IF I BELIEVE THAT I AM WORTHY OF CREATING A LIFE?

You may need to recall this sage advice: Fake it till you make it. Heart-provoking ideas:

ROLE MODELS: Mine are CQ, my friend Marcie, Susan B. Anthony, and Buddhist nun Pema Chodron.

KIND SELF-TALK: How do you talk to the people and animals you love? How do you speak to a child? Are you speaking to yourself with the same kindness?

SEASONAL: Sara sat outside several mornings and asked herself, "How can I co-create with the season outside my windows? She said, "The things I came up with were subtle: making a fall vegetable stew, taking a silent walk in the old cemetery near my house. . . . I mostly found myself with a sense of the changes happening around me. I felt more rooted and aware." Gather rocks and construct a fountain, walk in the rain, sleep outdoors, feed crumbs to ducks, learn the names for clouds.

What Is a
Comfort Queen?

"If I was to sit and ask, 'What do I need right now?' the answer would almost always be chocolate and coffee or a hot bath. Ninety percent of the time that's not what I really need." Saral laughs and pushes her blond braid behind her. "I need what is uncomfortable but what would bring me happiness. The distinction between pleasure and happiness is an important one. I believe three things are important: courage, patience, and commitment. Commitment would come into play here by being disciplined enough to picture the future. 'Is this going to bring me happiness a year from now?' That question helps me authenticate my inner knowing."

"We often do what feels *good* instead of what would be *best* for the overall development of our lives," Jennifer Freed agreed. "Those are not necessarily the same thing. When you are in touch with your inner wisdom or whatever you name it, then listening will ultimately make you feel better as well as give you what's best for you. At first you may have to go more for what's best for you than what feels good."

The distinctions that Saral and Jennifer make between happiness and pleasure, between what feels good and what would be best for our overall development, is a vital one. They have discovered the importance of going past the easy response, learning to name and then hold the tension of wanting two conflicting things: veg out in front of the TV *and* connect with your partner or make a lot of money *and* live an environmentally responsible, spiritually legitimate life, just two examples of the monumental and incremental conflicts that we face every day.

"Those gals have learned how to take care of themselves so that they can survive the anxiety and the fear that can come with choosing happiness. Comfort can get in the way of creating your life, or it can be the cuisine your stamina and courage feast on, the savory substance that fuels you when creating your life gets tough because it requires you to live your life fully."

I'm sitting in a local café, reading over my interviews and jotting down ideas in my journal. I surreptitiously glance around, expecting to see CQ striding through the room, crowned head held high. I spot a neighbor and wave halfheartedly. Maybe public places are off limits now that I have my own muse. Then I notice that the small teapot on my table has sprouted CQ's face. I hiss at her, "Who do you think you are, Angela Lansbury? This is not a Disney movie."

True to form, CQ ignores me and keeps talking. Thankfully, no one seems to notice her, and no white-coated attendants show up at my table. "I have no patience for people who define comfort or self-nurturing too narrowly. Take, for example, my moniker. Some people, upon hearing my name, mistake me for a gay man with excellent taste in bed linens. Others think I'm a woman who will not engage with the day unless it is 76 degrees outside and I've loofahed my cellulite, repeated my affirmations, done my yoga *and* cardio workout, exfoliated, journaled, tweezed, meditated, eaten a low-carbo, high protein, no wheat, no dairy breakfast, and donned an organic cotton outfit."

I chuckle and a few people do look over. I lean closer to CQ, pretending to check the pot for hot water, while I whisper, "Now that you mention it, you don't fit my image of a Comfort Queen. You're so much"—I search for the right word— "so much more durable."

"Durable? I've been called a lot of things . . ." She rolls her eyes, or at least tries. Porcelain lacks expressiveness. "'Durable' is rather drab but actually not too far off the mark. Comfort, in my definition, means to strengthen. And to soothe and befriend, ease and refresh. Queenly comes from the notion of divine right, the idea that queens were given the right to rule from the Divine and were accountable only to the Divine. In my rendition, I have been given the right to rule over my own life, and I'm definitely accountable to Ms. Holy Spirit, although not only to her. I consider myself accountable to others, but others of *my* choosing. Put it all together and you've got me. Write this in bold in that journal of yours":

Self-nurturing is more than pampering. It is about becoming powerful.

CQ continues, "Comforting yourself is about strengthening yourself, becoming, as you say, more durable. Then you can withstand the fear and discomfort that come calling when you choose to create your life, when you choose to be conscious and accountable."

I begin to understand that this guardian teapot of mine is about more than naps and essential oils. "How exactly do I do this?" I cautiously ask.

CQ studies me and I feel that I'm being assessed for readiness. "Ask yourself in the moment of fear, in the moment of wanting to escape, 'What would make me feel good while helping me dance with the fear of being fully alive?' This, of course, leads you right back to discernment."

"Discerning how to comfort myself?"

"Yes," answers CQ, "among other things. How many times have you asked for guidance and then become annoyed by what you heard?"

"I suppose a lot," I admit grudgingly as I toy with the sugar packs.

CQ hops a few inches across the table. Alarmed, I reach out and cover her with my hand. "Stop that, someone is going to see you."

She smiles. "I want to be sure I have your attention. Here's what I see you do, how you avoid both discernment and true listening. If you don't like what you hear when you ask for guidance, if it doesn't fit with what you lust after or are comfortable with, you disregard it. Toss it out. Or you seesaw in the other direction and decide that what you heard was infallible, a kind of inner Ouija board. Ms. Jennifer, you are basically a Ping-Pong ball, stopping a little bit to listen, then getting batted around by your fears and Ms. Resistance, then deciding that listening is completely reliable—spiritual Velcro."

"I hate to admit it, but you're right. You left out how I also simply forget to slow down long enough to truly listen. I let fifteen-second prayers and attempts at listening peter off into endless to-do lists."

CQ jiggles her pot lid and wags her spout at me. "To engage with life, you have to be in touch with your inner life. To be in touch with your inner life you have to listen. To listen, you have to be comfortable enough in your own skin so that you can discern what you are hearing." CQ gives her lid one more jiggle. "You'll get it." With a royal wave of her handle, my teapot becomes a teapot again. I hiss at her, "Hey, I'm not finished asking questions."

The teapot lid opens a crack and CQ says, rather loudly, "Keep asking—that's the whole point!" I notice several people trying not to stare at me. I decide it's time to go home.

"I don't think you can live in harmony with your inner knowing all the time," Saral had said when we talked about this a few days before. "My deepest knowing thinks that I should be in the middle of nowhere, on open land, part of the earth. I hear, 'This isn't the right place for me to live' all the time. But this is my husband's home; it is where he fits. There are times when that voice will tell me to do something and I have to make a decision whether I will or not, even if I know it is the right voice. It doesn't have to be 'I have to move tomorrow because I know this isn't the right place for me to live.' That's only one way to respond. But to balance that voice is tricky. If I balanced that voice with practicality, I would not have gone to Ashland, which changed my life. On the other hand, you do have to have another voice that says, 'I'm in the driver's seat.' I'm having a conversation with the voice that says I shouldn't live in Santa Barbara. I'm saying, 'I'm married and the man I'm married to wants to live here and we gotta work this out.'"

Blindly following what we hear can lead us into the arms of familiar but unhealthy behavior patterns. We must ask what the harvest of the Spirit will be if I follow this image/idea/voice? Am I being led toward peace and kindness, joy and love, patience toward my unfolding, toward fidelity and gentleness toward myself and those I love and respect? Or am I being led toward justification of poor behavior, controlling others, greed, ignoring the truth, an uneasy feeling in the pit of my stomach? A self-aggrandizing voice that suggests we are on course because we are getting what we want is probably not the voice we want to act on, is not leading us toward surrender.

Because surrendering to what we need to hear can be so difficult, we may need help getting to the place of wisdom that is greater than our need to be right or look as if we have it all together. Nora Gallagher, an author and an Episcopal postulant in the process of discerning a vocation to the priesthood, tells a beautiful story of sitting with a group of priests, spiritual directors, and her bishop at Mount Calvary monastery and participating in an exercise called the Listening Stick. "Someone hands you a stick and says, 'Go inside yourself and find the question that needs to be asked,'" Nora explains. "Then I ask that question of the person sitting on my right, and he answers my question. Because it was very soon after my brother died, I asked, 'What has been the most significant death for you?' The person on my right was a priest. He went inside himself to find his answer. He told a story about his first assignment as a chaplain, attending the death of a young man whose heart transplant didn't take. We all listened until he got to the end of the story. When you're focused on someone, listening until he gets to the end of his story, he *gets* to the end. He has a complete thought. It was very profound. The activity of asking the question and truly answering it, giving yourself time to answer, is a very healing process. It's very small, but it's very important. None of us really do it much, for others or ourselves; we don't get to the end. We don't get to the completed, final place where it's all done."

Nora also sat in a questioning circle as part of her explorations into being ordained. "I went through a discernment committee," she said. "The committee would sit in silence for maybe an hour until someone was moved to ask a question. It could be asked of me or of the group. We never talked about what provoked the question. It would become obvious that a question was coming up. It was wonderful to sit with other people for so long, to hear and wait for something to come up." What would it be like if you brought your listening into such a group?

We must never forget the potent and reliable wisdom of the body as an excellent authenticator and helper in times of confusion. The ideas and images you can trust resonate with the clarity of a single chime in perfect tune with your body. As you are listening, pay attention to your delicate internal sensations. A positive direction expresses itself as a subtle release, perhaps in your solar plexus or your forehead or as an overall sense of ease. Being off the mark, or heading in the wrong direction might feel like a tightening in your chest or a hunching of your shoulders or a clenching of your hands. With a little practice, your body can become a fine-tuned indicator of which voices to heed and which to gently put aside.

Graphic artist Devon uses another question to test her perceptions, "Am I altering or avoiding a decision to seek approval or make others happy? That's the watershed question for me, the dead giveaway that I'm off track and need to go back to square one. Of course, sometimes I know I'm doing something to please people and I do it anyway. But I find power even in that knowing."

You could ask a question one day and receive one answer and ask the same question another day and get a different answer. That's the way life's supposed to be. The ultimate authority is you. Yet you have to be sober enough to ask, "Am I kidding myself? Am I not kidding myself?" As Saral said, "If I'm not sure of my knowing, I'm going to get a lot of information to compare and weigh. I talk to other people. And then I go into retreat space and listen some more. Asking again,

'What is my truth? What is my real knowing? What's my bullshit knowing?' It often takes time to grasp the answer. We want it in five minutes."

What if we hear nothing but noise? We can examine our diet (cut down on sugar, carbohydrates, and caffeine) and we can accept confusion as "an opportunity for your true self to appear" as Robert Johnson says in his book *Contentment*: "Instead of rushing to remove confusion, try approaching it as rich with potential. Don't be in such a hurry to chase away these moments through willful action. Try to sit with your confusion, to go more deeply into it with an attitude of expectation. Patiently hold the tension of not knowing." Holding the tension of not knowing leads us into CQ's territory, into taking good enough care of ourselves so that we are able to sit with the skin-crawling, head-popping anxiety and fear of not knowing what to do, of not being sure of what we are hearing, of not being sure we will live our lives fully, and not only survive these feelings but thrive.

Sometimes it is not confusion or terror that greets us but silence. That too requires patience. The patience to ask, What else do I need to learn before I can ask? Perhaps you need to gather more information. The patience to do nothing and ask again a few days later. The patience to reformulate your question, perhaps into something more open-ended. The patience to accept paradox.

I never said this was going to be easy.

"And I never said it couldn't be fun." CQ appears carrying a pile of fluffy towels and two beach chairs. "Stop worrying so much about discerning and authenticating and all those big Jungian words. It's practice you need. Let's go practice at the beach."

I start to say, "But I have so much work to do," but CQ waves her scepter and what comes out of my mouth is, "Sounds divine. Let's pick up Lilly at her friend's house on our way." The response in my body is pure release, a colossal *Ahhh*. CQ even makes me feel good about wearing a bathing suit.

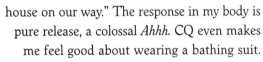

WHAT DAILY PRINCIPLE AM I ORGANIZING MY LIFE AROUND?

When I asked women this question, I got responses like "obligation," "tea and toast," "my kids," "work," and "making money." These are very real, but there needs to be more. Gratitude, listening to Mystery, a creative act, yoga, prayer, whatever speaks to you.

WHAT DO I KEEP TELLING MYSELF WILL BE OKAY, OR WHAT REALITY AM I IGNORING?

Mimi kept telling herself her parents would get their financial affairs together some-day. Babs ignored her body's need for downtime. Natalie disregarded the long silences between her and her partner. Devon managed to put off grieving the loss of her father by starting a new business. For now, see if you can name what is crooking a finger at you from under the stairs.

WHAT IS ONE THING I COULD DO TO NURTURE THREE IMPORTANT PEOPLE IN MY LIFE?

Partner, best friend, grandmother. What do you really want to do? Keep it small, invite silliness, invite risk, open your heart. Do not invite overdoing or more than three people.

Reward

By now you may have completed the seven pages of questions. My definition of *complete* includes *glanced at for a few seconds* or *written opuses about*. Remember, there is no one way. And it doesn't matter if you spent a month or two years exploring these questions. All that matters is that you honored yourself by listening. That you chose to bestow awareness on your life.

Can you give yourself a reward? Not later, not tomorrow, *now*. Something robust or subtle, solitude or togetherness, a leap of faith or a self-cuddling.

Do you feel remarkable enough to continue to give yourself this attention, to cultivate your awareness? Remember, you can always put your hair shirt back on. Whom do you want to emulate? Thelma and Louise (without the murder and mayhem) or Jane Hathaway in *The Beverly Hillbillies*? Or queenly you with perhaps a little self-kindness and awareness draped around your luscious shoulders?

The choice is yours.

Do you value yourself enough to look at the life burning within you? The love that you bestow on others, can you bestow it on yourself? Can you fling away the false modesty that puts self-love second? Can you use this questioning process in this spirit? Can I?

HOW AM I SPENDING MY TIME IN A WAY THAT DOESN'T SUPPORT ME?

I found my way out of the pit of despair partly by recognizing how easily distracted I am. Stopping myself from talking on the phone, eating snacks, or checking e-mail during my writing time was very difficult at first, but *choosing* to stay put in my chair was what I needed.

WHAT MESSAGE AM I SENDING THE UNIVERSE?

Reflect on the sum of your attitudes and actions in the last month or so. CQ pops up to add, "If you were a radio tower beaming signals into infinity, would you be transmitting life-affirming beacons or poison pellets of self-loathing? If there was a huge reflecting dish out in space, would you need to wear a helmet to protect yourself from what it would beam back at you?"

WHAT AM I WILLING TO PRAISE MYSELF FOR?

Acceptance, forgiveness, and praise are the shock absorbers on the path to living a conscious life. It is often exceedingly difficult to praise ourselves. But by praising even infinitesimal things about ourselves or our lives, we develop aplomb and intensify essence. In the beginning, if you can't find anything to praise, pretend. In a few tries, pretending will plant roots and grow true feeling. Try listing a few accomplishments, no matter how diminutive.

Living the Questions

continued

WHAT NEGATIVE ATTITUDES OR BELIEFS DO I WANT TO HOLD ON TO, AT LEAST FOR NOW?

The Buddhist nun and author Pema Chodron says there is nothing wrong with being negative. The problem arises when we think negative thoughts and then feel guilty about them.

CAN I ALLOW MYSELF TO BE NEGATIVE WITHOUT FEELING GUILTY?

CQ adds, "This is a cagey one, this being negative without wallowing, being truthful with where you are. Try this exercise: Imagine a beautiful tray. Imagine laying out on this tray everything you feel negative about. Put it all out, very carefully, and give it a calm look-see. No need to change it and no need to carry it with you today."

It Is Possible

"I remember when that moment came, when I made a decision to, if not so much to create my life, then to be the caretaker of it." Jan didn't look at me as she spoke but toward her ten-month-old baby, Emma, whom she was giving a bath. "It wasn't very long ago, maybe four years. It was spring. You always remember the seasons here." Jan nods at the bare trees outside her suburban Illinois window. "What triggered this shift for me was reading a book called *Divided Lives*. I was living what looked like a fine life, working as an associate professor at a progressive community college. My first daughter was two, my marriage was good, and we even had enough money. But I always felt two steps behind the music, as if I was running to catch up. When I talked to my girlfriends about this feeling, we all chalked it up to not having enough: enough time, enough support, enough of us to go around. It was a vague feeling, and it *wasn't* that feeling of 'Is this all there is?' It was a feeling of not being enough."

How intimately we all know Phantom Not-Good-Enough. She's the biggest obstacle, besides economic inequality and inadequate support for families, that prevents us from creating our lives. The monkey on our back, the manacle on our spirit, the horse in the open stall who refuses to run free. How many times had I been asked, "How will I ever make time for myself?" and tried to convince the woman asking that the answer was "When you believe you deserve it." Jan mentioned this. "It sounds so simplistic, but a few years ago I woke up to the fact that I have to create my life or someone else will do it for me, probably in a way I won't like. The point is, *I thought I was awake.*" Jan points to the bookshelves that line a small alcove off the living room. I rummage around there until I find a copy of *Divided Lives* by Elsa Walsh. "I forgot about my capacity to choose. Go ahead, read that part about Dr. Alison Eastbrook."

Divided Lives covers a period of time in the lives of three prominent and accomplished women, women whom Walsh chose because they "enjoyed all the advantages of wealth, education, and opportunity, and who had broken through barriers traditionally viewed as male... and still had trouble creating balanced and satisfying lives." Dr. Alison Eastbrook is one of the three women Walsh spent years interviewing. Eastbrook struggles within the chauvinistic surgery department of Columbia Presbyterian Medical Center in New York City. The story begins with Alison discovering she is making $40,000 less a year than the two male residents hired at the same time she was and then follows her struggles to remain chief of the breast clinic after she is appointed.

Jan interrupts from the kitchen, where she is preparing dinner: "One week these male doctors say Alison is the chief of the breast clinic; the next week they are conducting a search for a more famous male candidate, and they do this, on and off, for two years. I want to strangle the men who decide that she isn't good enough to be chief simply because she is a woman. But I want to strangle Allison, too. Why doesn't she stand up for herself? Why is she killing herself bringing in a million dollars a year in billable hours instead of protesting?" Jan punctuates her words with jabs of her chopping knife. "I was able to see my own life in Alison's story. She is running faster and faster trying to prove herself. She does not believe she has any other choice. Nothing changes until she sees that she does, *until she values herself enough to ask for help.* When she does that, male doctors call off the search and her worries are over within a day. I remember wondering if it could be that easy." Jan comes back into the living room and hands me a plate of carrot and celery sticks. "If I don't make the decision, over and over again to pilot my own life, to ask for help, to stand up for myself, no one else will. It sounds so obvious, but what I got from Alison's story is that it *isn't* obvious. I think I am creating my life until I look deeper; then I find I am still running on the assumption that I'm not quite good enough to do so." Jan glances at me, struggling to articulate her elusive feelings. "I feel like I've woken up from a deep sleep or that something snapped in me. I'm trying not to be overzealous, but I know now I deserve to pilot my own life." She grins and fluffs her hair. "It's L'Oréal and I'm worth it."

CQ lets loose a rebel yell that jerks me back into the present from recounting my visit with Jan. I follow her ululation to the backyard, where she is once again flying through the air on Lilly's swing. "I like that Jan. She has found the gogo juice every woman needs: the belief that you can do it. And I love this swing. It has such an extravagant arc."

I walk down the stairs. By the time I get to CQ, she has arranged a café table and pitcher of iced tea. We rest in the shade of our oak trees. I look around our neglected but beautiful yard, profoundly grateful I no longer live in the middle of a vast city. "I've been out in this yard more in the last few weeks then I have in the last two years."

CQ pours me some tea. "Having a comfort queen around will do that to you. Let's talk about the belief that you deserve to come out here and sit, even when I'm not around."

"CQ, you are preaching to the choir," I protest. "I've never had any trouble believing I deserve whatever a man has. If anything, as some people would testify, I've been rather rabid about being equal."

CQ shakes the teapot at me. "I didn't say anything about being equal to a man. A sense of deserving can't be compared to anyone else. It has to spring from inside you. It has to be as unshakable and immutable as the earth. It's the piece that unlocks the rest of creating your life: I can."

In M.F.K. Fisher's memoir *The Gastronomical Me*—which I discovered thanks to Carol Flinders's book *At the Root of This Longing*—there is a modest but thrilling moment when Mary Frances overcomes her painful shyness and self-consciousness and learns to ask for what she wants. It happens, not surprisingly, over a meal. She has been traveling by train with her uncle, bound from Los Angeles to Chicago. Her uncle has been coaching her on how to order exactly what she wants to eat, building up her verve and mettle, her "I can." When they reach Chicago, however, they are joined by his nearly grown son and M.F.K. falls back into shyness, casting her eyes into her lap and whispering, "Anything will do" when the waiter arrives with a menu. But then she happens to look up and catch her uncle's eye, and something clicks. "I knew that it was a very important time in my life. I looked at my menu, really looked with all my brain, for the first time. 'Just a minute, please,' I said, very calmly. I stayed quite cool, like a surgeon when he begins an operation, or maybe a chess player opening a tournament. Finally I said to Uncle Evans, without batting an eye, 'I'd like iced consommé, please, and then sweetbreads *sous cloche* and a watercress salad . . . and I'll order the rest later.' I remember he sat back in his chair a little, and I knew that he was proud of me and very fond of me too. I was too."

The right to create our lives is constantly being eroded and challenged. We can easily become numb to the challenge and, little by little, retreat from our belief in ourselves, unaware that we are conforming to another's expectations. In Nuala O'Faolain's memoir *Are You Somebody?,* she writes, "I never stood back and looked at myself and what I was doing. I didn't value myself enough—take myself seriously enough—to reflect even privately on whether my existence had any pattern, any meaning. . . . Yet my life burned inside me. Even such as it was, it was the only record of me, and it was my only creation, and something in me would not accept that it was insignificant. Something in me must have been waiting to stand up and demand to be counted." I was bowled over by the image of Nuala careening through her life, never stopping to learn from the patterns that had formed behind her. She shows us how easy it is to fall asleep at the wheel. It is in stopping to perceive the pattern that we discern what we are creating, and can determine if it is what we want to create.

CQ raises her cup to me. "Her only creation demanded to be counted. You have to wake yourself up to that truth over and over again. A toast to it is possible." We both say "Brava" as our cups clink.

I sip before I venture to ask, "And how *do* you wake yourself up over and over again?"

CQ grins. "Fierce desire, my friend. An intimate and fiery relationship with fierce desire is what it takes." She waggles her eyebrows at me. I grin in anticipation.

IF I COULD DO OR BE OR FEEL ANYTHING
IN THE COMING DAYS, WHAT WOULD IT BE?

Unencumbered	Close to the Divine	Determined
Sexy	Proud	Responsible for only me
Wild	Accomplished	Or . . . ?
Instinctual	Focused	
Relaxed	Strong	

IF I COULD DO OR BE OR FEEL ANYTHING WITH SOMEONE
CLOSE TO ME, WHAT WOULD I CHOOSE?

Connected	Understood	Fascinated	Queen-like	Vulnerable
Silly	Belly laugh	Friendly	Patient	Or . . . ?
At peace	Decisive	Seductive	Luminous	
Heard	Inventive	Feminine	Clear	

AM I WILLING TO TRY? CAN I GIVE MYSELF AT
LEAST A TASTE OF WHATEVER IT IS I'VE DREAMED UP?

What do you need to wake up to, risk, reach for, or let go of? Say you want to feel a job well done after you turn in a report at work. What aren't you doing yet that you need to do to have that feeling? Or perhaps you want to go biking for a week with friends but you are neither in good enough shape nor do you have the time or money. Could you bike for one hour on Sunday for a taste of your dream? Or maybe you want to feel decisive with your work team. What would you have to say? Wear? Believe?

CQ appears on your shoulder, a tiny queen. She whispers in your ear, "My darling, let yourself have a taste. I've broken open the box. You're free. Savor that taste. Or gulp it and demand more." She pats you on the cheek. Perhaps you let yourself sigh.

Fierce Desire

It seemed as essential and invisible as water to a fish: create your life or your life will create you. Make the daily decision to be the agent of your own life.

As if it were that simple. There is that tiny detail of the meltdown that almost always comes first, before you can be an agent of your life. You must first reach the place where you want it badly enough, where you are willing to make the difficult choices that creating a life *always* necessitates. It seems most of us have to be in enough pain, hop over enough hot coals, before we can give birth to fierce desire. Through hardship, depression, divorce, a failed career, midlife crisis, spiritual practice, political work, out of the tenderizing experiences of life, emerges the determination to listen to the life that is yours, no matter what the cost. To find and, if necessary, fight for the life that reflects your soul, the life you will be at peace with when you turn and look back.

Read women's biographies and you see fierce desire being born. Relentless sexism birthed that fierce desire in Dr. Alison Eastbrook—she learned to fight for what she had worked for. Georgia O'Keeffe was almost pulled to pieces by the conflict between what her husband wanted and what she needed to survive. Out of that conflict sprang her yearly trips to New Mexico and the turning point of her life's work: Georgia had to learn to disappoint others—what woman who wants to create her life hasn't? Saint Catherine of Genoa, wanting desperately to be free of her social and marital obligations to pursue her devotion to God, prayed to be sick for three months so she would be left alone. This may not seem like fierce desire to us, but it *fit* Saint Catherine. It fit the shape of her life. Our fierce desire has to fit *us.* Fierce desire is never what we are supposed to do, no matter where the definition of prescribed behavior comes from. If it doesn't jibe with what we know to be true and right for us, it's wrong.

While one woman I interviewed, author Beth Wilson, has had this fierce desire her entire life, she was the exception. More typical was my neighbor Bridget. Bridget experienced her own dark night of the soul and emerged to *decide* to live a life based on self-nurturing and self-kindness. An exemplary overachiever, she not only ran her own business but took care of her aging mother and was very involved in her church. It was with Bridget that I clearly saw the connection between the decision to create our lives and self-nurturing. She did not take care of herself. She did not easily let others take care of her. Bridget began to hide at home, depressed, considering divorce, becoming as thin as a cartoon turned sideways. By paying attention to and listening to her despair, she came to understand that the only way she could *live* was to make the decision to care for herself. Before her dark time, when I offered to help her in some small way, Bridget would have refused or accepted only a portion of what was offered. Now she was calling me and asking me for help. She was claiming Saturday mornings as her day off. When I last spoke to her, she was taking off for a weekend yoga retreat, something she would never have considered before.

Bridget reached the point where she had to choose: Do I value myself enough to create a life worth living or not? More than deciding to do something for herself, Bridget had tapped the reason *why she was doing what she was doing with her life.* Not the meaning of life, because that isn't something we can label. Instead, she found a way to have constant contact with the *sense,* the feeling of purpose that we all crave. Bridget found her route to this sense through yoga, questions, time in nature, *and* through the *conviction* that this communication is indispensable for her survival. On the surface, it may simply look as if she is making yoga a priority, making more time for herself. What is really happening is that Bridget and many other women are understanding that self-nurturing is *not* an occasional fluffy reward, something you give yourself after a bad day, but a route to finding meaning and sustaining the courage to follow that meaning.

CQ appears outside my window, watering my pansies. "Write this in capitals, shout it from the rooftops":

THE DECISION TO CREATE YOUR LIFE MUST BE BASED IN SELF-KINDNESS AND FED BY SELF-NURTURING.

"Creating a life without self-kindness isn't creating a life, it's sandpainting. First windy day and it's all gone." CQ pinches my pansies back and then attacks the aphids on my rosebush. "Lots of women have been creating their lives for the last thirty years, but they have been doing it from a place of desperation, ego, slave driving, or trying to prove something that did need to be proved. A lot of that has been necessary. During a revolution, you have to swing far to one side in order to capture new freedoms."

Why bother to create our lives if we don't value them in the first place? If we are constantly flogging ourselves, we cannot sustain the energy we need to make the decision, over and over again, to stand up for ourselves and to stretch toward wholeness. Every woman I have interviewed or read about who feels good in her skin is able to do so because she values herself. It was a value learned through struggle, study of other women's lives, and spiritual experience. These women breathe the belief that they're worth it. Like a friend who said that despite the severe hardships she had faced in her early life, she never hated herself because she knew God loved her, and if God loved her, how could she hate herself?

I look outside at CQ and she nods. "You're tying it together. Creating your life is not a linear process; it's circles within spirals. Value yourself enough to choose to create your life. But how do you value yourself? By treating yourself like some-one you love. How do you do that? By nurturing yourself in a way that helps you stay awake and keep choosing to create your life."

"And do all this while dancing backward in high heels," I tease.

CQ answers with a provocative shake of her hips and then a flourish of an Irish jig. She dances until her nose is against my window screen and she's locked eyes with me. "Are you willing to dance backward, although thank God you don't have to do it in high heels anymore? Jenny, my darling, have you decided you're worth it? Because there is, strangely enough, a fine peace in saying no. Readiness is crucial. Ripeness is crucial."

Am I ready? Am I ripe? Am I worth it? This was something I decided long ago but Jan was right. This decision to create your life, to value yourself enough, had to be made over and over again.

I stand up. "CQ, I'm ripe and ready to fall from the tree."

WHAT ONE THING AM I WILLING TO KNOW ABOUT MY LIFE RIGHT NOW?

Take a moment right now to go inside and ask yourself this question. CQ says, "Honey, I know going inside isn't easy, I know Ms. Anxiety and Colonel Fear are knocking at your door right about now and they are saying, 'You don't really want to know anything about your life, do you?' But you declare, 'Yes, I do.' Let it come. Trust yourself to hear just what you need to hear and no more. Take it slow and easy."

AM I MAKING MY LIFE MORE DIFFICULT OR COMPLICATED THAN IT NEEDS TO BE?

Jan realized she didn't need to make a complicated casserole for the faculty dinner; she went to the store and bought her potluck dish. After listening to herself, Dorsey said no to being president of the board of a Shakespeare festival she had helped establish. Her two young sons would finally both be in school, and she wanted time to write.

HOW CAN I NURTURE MY BELOVED SELF?

BASIC PHYSICAL CARE: Lots of water, a long walk with time for stretching, enough sleep for an entire week, healthy food . . .

SPIRITUAL SUSTENANCE: Attend a church, meditate and write in your journal for a morning with two friends, read a spiritual classic with your partner outside in the moonlight . . .

EMOTIONAL RELEASE: Set a timer for fifteen minutes, put on music, lie on the couch, and give yourself up to the feelings that emerge.

AM I WILLING TO DO ANY OF THESE THINGS FOR MYSELF IN THE NEXT WEEK?

Fear of Being Self-Absorbed

How many of us are afraid that if self-nurturing becomes our way of being, we won't ever get off the couch again? If pleasure and joy become our way of life, won't we slack off and never amount to anything? Won't we end up stealing bottles from other people's recycling containers, rattling down the street behind our shopping cart with seventeen skinny cats trailing behind our flea-bitten ankles? Or might we become indolent gluttons with chocolate dribbling down our chins, running through the streets naked, begging, "More, more, more"?

"It's always a possibility. But I think not." Hanging over my desk is a small wooden carving from Bali of a woman with wings, a tail, and a golden headdress. A moment ago she was a block of ornately carved wood. Now her lips are moving. CQ has possessed my Indonesian angel.

"How's Bali these days?" I inquire politely, proud of my aplomb.

"Exquisite. The Balinese know quite a bit about true pleasure."

I lean back in my chair to better see her and to avoid getting a crick in my neck. "I suspect you're going to enlighten me as to what true pleasure is?"

CQ bats her wooden eyelashes. "We've already discussed the need for discernment. What we didn't get into, because you weren't ready, is shadow comfort."

My foot nervously begins to tap the floor. Shadow comforts are encumbrances, like eating too many sweets, watching too much TV, shopping for things we don't need, surfing the Internet, reading too much—numbing out. Another name for these types of behavior is "soft addictions," or "buffers." I might as well mention time monsters while I'm at it, shadow comforts' first cousins. Time monsters are anything or anyone who eats our time and takes us away from what is worthwhile, juicy, and meaningful. Procrastination is a big time monster. Reading the newspaper or fashion magazines for the sake of getting caught up, overzealous record keeping that has no payoff, phone conversations with people we don't really want to talk to, pointless meetings with unprepared people. Over the years, I've been good at writing about shadow comforts and time monsters while managing to ignore the slimy creatures in my own life. The speed of my foot tapping increases.

CQ studies me. "Shadow comfort doesn't nourish you; it diminishes you. It's what many people think of when they think of comfort. They are actually punishing themselves instead of nourishing their souls."

"But shadow comforts are so satisfying, so familiar. And time monsters are so compelling," I counter.

CQ's tone is gentle. "Once you understand pleasure, you won't say that. When you don't know what truly gives you pleasure, you are left with sneaky, guilty substitutions. Genuine hunger is a wise teacher."

"I feel I need to rely on willpower to stay away from shadow comforts. After a while, the discipline of staying away from those things breaks down, and I go off the deep end, which does not make me feel good." I pick up a pencil and doodle a picture of a flower opening. "When that happens, my critical voice has a field day. 'See what happens when you take care of yourself. You can't be trusted. Stick with work and routine, and you'll be safe.' It's all so confusing and tedious."

I feel CQ's eyes on me, but I look at my paper and keep doodling. "Overdoing it, indulgences that don't satisfy, and narcissism are all related to emptiness, boredom, and self-hatred," CQ tells me. "Shadow comforts and time monsters are fed by the inability to trust yourself enough to go into the hunger and listen to it. But when you connect with your fierce desire, when you value yourself enough to savor the life bubbling through your veins, and when you *continually* listen, then the potential for narcissistic self-absorption and destructive indulgences shrinks dramatically. It becomes easier both to trust yourself and to be good to yourself. Nurturing yourself and nurturing others are not mutually exclusive. It's another circle within a spiral."

I glance at her. "All these spirals and circles are snarling my synapses."

CQ ignores my sarcasm. "As you become more loving toward yourself, you are more able to listen to the needs of others. You are more able to leave behind the illusion that your life is more in need of care and attention than anyone else's because you are meeting your own needs, at least some of the time."

"You make it sound easy. Insert tab A into slot B, as seen on TV, and balanced self-love will be yours," I protest. But CQ is gone.

I sit gazing out the window at the neighbor's driveway and the glimpse of mountains beyond, thinking about the many swings in attitude I had observed in women who had taken on self-nurturing as a way of being: rigid defensiveness (especially in the beginning when we don't trust ourselves to say no or to protect our precious resources of time and energy, we can hold everyone off with a ten-foot-I'm-nurturing-myself pole); a holier than thou demeanor (I'm taking care of myself, why aren't you?); and plain garden-variety self-absorption (Enough about me. Tell me, what do you think of me? Oh, is that a body cast you're wearing? But what do you think of *my* outfit?). And then there were the hazy gray areas—Was I self-indulgent when I went to a movie last Wednesday instead of spending another hour and half before bed with Lilly? Yes, somewhat. True, I desperately needed a break, a mental escape from a pressing problem that was weighing on me. Yet I noticed I wasn't willing to look and listen to see if she needed me more than I needed a break. I wanted to check out more than I wanted to listen to her needs. Warning: woman in process, wear your hard hat.

When we hit a tennis ball smack in the middle of our racket, we know we've hit the sweet spot and we feel it throughout our body. Hitting on a self-loving and self-respecting attitude feels the same. This feeling can be our homing device. Smack! I'm in the middle of my sweet spot. You feel more you, more awake, clearer about giving and receiving. The more you hit your sweet spot, the more this fear of being a petty, venal, hoggish caricature of a self-nurturing woman fades away. (Okay, she might not fade away *immediately,* but she will fade. Give it time.)

Surprise! It all comes back to listening. It is what, coupled with experience, helps us navigate the gray areas, tease out self-acceptance, love of life, and real pleasure instead of denial, narcissism, and guilty, unsatisfying substitutes. An ardently self-indulgent woman is rarely willing to stop and listen, to look at the whole of her life. An ardently self-indulgent woman luxuriates in her self-importance, cell phone humming, surrounding herself with proof of how indispensable she is. Remember, it's *easier* to be busy. You don't have to connect, with others or yourself.

Mary Davies frames it this way: "It's so easy to get confused about life when it's divided into work and pleasure, when we think we need to slot in payback time for everything we push ourselves to achieve. I'm thinking about some kind of integration, where everything is God's and mine together." What would it be like if we viewed each day as a creation? What if we decided we were creating our *opus dei,* for someone or something larger than ourselves, the greater good of womankind or the Divine? Everything could become meaningful and purposeful, awash with marvelous possibility.

Living in the self-love zone, emulating CQ, is like owning our TV set. We don't have cable, so to pick up a signal Chris or I spend a fair amount of time adjusting the rabbit ears on top of the set. Sometimes one of us has to keep a body part connected to the TV, say a leg stretched out, to keep the reception unscrambled. It takes patience, creativity, agility, and a fierce desire to see *Masterpiece Theater.*

Self-absorbed women may have the agility, but they definitely lack these other abilities.

What kind of reception are you picking up?

WHAT IS THE ONE THING I NEED
MORE OF IN MY LIFE RIGHT NOW?

Grace	Organization	Eating exactly what
Self-kindness	Determination	my body wants
Movement	Wildness	Time to think
Silliness	Touch	Fill in the blank: ____
Doodling	Nature	

Pick the *one* thing you *need* most.

WHAT ONE OR TWO MODEST STEPS AM I WILLING TO TAKE
TO GET MORE _____ IN MY LIFE?

In yoga, the smallest adjustments can change the feeling of the whole pose. So can breathing into a place that is fearful or tight.

WHAT HAVE I ALLOWED MYSELF
TO RECEIVE IN THE LAST FEW DAYS?

A compliment, a feeling of being appreciated, an offer of help, no matter how small?

WHAT DO I WISH I HAD LET MYSELF RECEIVE?

CQ wraps her rose-colored cashmere shawl around you and rubs your shoulders. "Here you are, you divine thing. Here you are, taking the time to build your life from the inside out. Let yourself be proud."

The Unfolding Path

We have to be careful with this idea of creating our lives. We can easily mix up a heady cocktail of self-importance with a control-freak chaser. We might find ourselves hiking to the top of a mountain and shouting, "I'm queen of the world," modeling ourselves after Leona Helmsley instead of CQ or someone of your own choosing whom you admire and trust. We can get carried away with the idea of fierce desire and decide that knowing what we want means getting it.

To create your life implies the ability, like Captain Picard on *Star Trek: The Next Generation,* to wave a hand and say, "Make it so." Next to Patrick Stewart's enticingly bald head, that was my favorite part of the series. "Make it so." To create is to cause to exist; bring into being. Do we bring ourselves into being? I fervently hope not. Sounds like far too much work. I'm more the barn-raising kind of gal. I want to work together.

There has to be a middle ground.

"Yes, the middle way. The inner force you saw in Nuala O'Faolain's decision to write her memoirs, to study the story of her life. That's what you need to follow." CQ appears as a saffron-colored mist swirling near one of my bookcases. I'm not only getting used to her interruptions, I look forward to them. What a writer won't do to procrastinate! "Follow the middle way," CQ repeats. "Follow the middle way."

"You sound like Glinda the Good Witch."

"For pity's sake, expand your cultural references beyond TV sitcoms and children's books." She disappears. I start looking for someone to shed light on the "middle way."

I find the person I need in the form of Carolyn Atkinson, acupuncturist and longtime student of Buddhism. Carol generously sheds light on this creating/control issue: "I used to think creating a life might or should be possible. But as I live life—and learn and suffer!—I'm concluding that I'm not so sure. Learning to be graceful and intentional with what comes our way, *learning how to recognize our life as it's happening to* us. For example, I think the early child-rearing years are hell for a lot of good parents because they also want to be doing so many other things—I know I did—career, writing, et cetera. I kept struggling to do the other things when I might have done better to be more graceful with what was happening around me. Struggling didn't change anything—it just made me unhappy. Which is not to say I shouldn't have done anything else [in addition to parenting]. No, not that. But it would have been possible to be happier if I'd accepted what was happening a little sooner and not tried to force my will all the time. So the trick is that 'creating a life'—the idea—can sometimes be a setup for forcing our will, instead of noticing what is. We each have our unique path to walk in this life. *We need not believe we have to create the path out of nothing,* but simply slow down enough to see the path as it unfolds before us. I've come more and more to the place of creative waiting that, to me, is the source of creating a life. It is in the waiting and the paying attention, and not in the action.

What happens is if we try to take control, we miss what's really happening. Then at some point there will be a collision between what we want and what's actually coming into being, what's getting ready to be born."

Carolyn's comments intrigued me greatly—learning how to recognize our life as it's happening to us. I had known for a long time that forcing my will was a bad idea. I had done that more than a few times and had paid a huge price, both literally and figuratively. Yet I found myself feeling uneasy. I thought about Dr. Alison Eastbrook. She didn't need to let her life unfold; she needed to protect what had already unfolded. What would happen if I followed this advice? Would I let others walk all over me? Would I never finish anything?

Monica Relph-Wikman, psychologist and astrologer, gave me the next piece I needed. "I'm confused over how I negotiate between creating my life—say, standing up for myself or setting goals—and watching my path unfold," I told her. She launched right in: "I can appreciate that, Jennifer. There is a tension between using your active consciousness, which wants to move, create, manage life, and set goals, and serving the life that's already in you, allowing your essence to unfold. This essence has its own dynamics and its own personality. I would say the essential way to create a life would be to do it in sync with how the soul wants to express itself through you. Which is not up to the ego. Staying in sync with what the deeper layers are asking, paying attention to larger energies, and using the will to express those, to create the life that this deeper place in you wants, is ultimately the most satisfying journey."

Robert Johnson described his way of approaching life in his memoir, *Balancing Heaven and Earth:* "The concept of listening to the will of God is difficult for many modern people to follow, as it collides with our love of freedom and our insistence on free will. . . . We all have free will, and therefore we can try to force situations in life. Perhaps that struggle is what keeps us bound to this earth. But I have gradually learned to accept that the slender threads [what Robert calls the guiding hand of an intelligent entity] possess greater intelligence and wisdom than our scrambling egos can ever attain. In good times and bad, one slender thread after another has seen me through and, together, they have shaped what I know and who I am. . . . I have learned to trust the slender threads for the big decisions in my life while using my ego to take care of the small details."

"Come take a walk with me." CQ has assumed a solid form and is wearing a workout outfit that would have made Flo Jo blush. I pull on a jacket and follow her into the foggy afternoon.

I can barely keep up with CQ's long legs. "Think about what happened when you first tried to write stories, fifteen years ago," she says. "You tried to figure out what would sell and then write a story based on that. You never could do it. You got yourself stuck more than once trying to do that. But when an idea grew slowly from within, in ephemeral images and dreamy fragments, with you doing plenty of stopping and listening, and not forcing it, those stories ended up being the best stories you ever wrote, even though you didn't think so because they never sold."

I nod yes and lengthen my stride. "What you are saying reminds me of one of my favorite books, *Fearless Creating* by Eric Maisel. I have this quote taped up by my computer: 'If you are to create, you must invite anxiety in. But then you must manage it.' I remember thinking, How liberating! To know my anxiety, the jittery undertow to my creative life, was *normal*. That feeling anxious is a normal part of creating a life. I find that thought very comforting." I give a little leap of happiness.

CQ points out three pileated woodpeckers on a riddled telephone pole. "One of the greatest ways to kill a creative life is to try to know too soon, to take an unfamiliar feeling, idea, or impulse and instantly morph it into something familiar and safe. To create a life worth living you have to be willing to do the two-step with Anxiety. You have to make friends with her. She bites her nails and she's not someone you'd want to sit through a three-hour Bergman film with, but she's a blast at a Stones concert. Bottom line: To create your life, you have to learn to like or at least tolerate being uncomfortable."

CQ stops and leans down to my eye level, gazing at me with an intensity I would usually find uncomfortable, but for some reason, today I welcome it. "Ms. Anxiety is very close with Colonel Fear, and he's the one you're really avoiding. You won't believe the lengths I've seen people go to avoid sitting down and having a talk with their fears. Root canals, IRS investigations, family reunions, you name it. Yet when we avoid Fear, he ends up running our lives, and we end up suffering. You have to want to create your life, you have to want to be fully alive more than you want to be comfortable. Put the two together and you have a lovely paradox." CQ hands me a chocolate kiss. "It's important to keep your strength up when exercising." We walk on in silent, reverent chocolate worship.

Whenever I write, I must sidle up next to Anxiety, allow her to test my courage and determination. I have to grow quiet inside, what Maisel calls "hushing and holding," so that thoughts, observations, ideas, can come. If they do come, I have to stop myself from launching into action. I have to be willing to hang out in the void—a very uncomfortable place. I was in the shower one day, where I get my best ideas, and I had a thought. I can't even remember what it was. What I do remember is I watched myself go from having the idea to developing it to being wildly successful with it to getting bored with it, all in the space of about two seconds. I didn't let the idea ripen. I stunted it by leaping ahead to what I wanted to happen. If, instead, I make friends with Anxiety, if I can use comfort and lean on CQ to help me with Anxiety, then I can open myself to what might be, what the larger energies of life might want to direct me toward. Which, I realized with a gulp, led me face-to-face with Fear.

CQ hands me another chocolate kiss. "First work with Anxiety. Teach her to leap. Otherwise you set yourself up for disappointment. You end up using your energy to deny her instead of to sustain your courage, and that won't help you with Fear at all."

"Teach her to leap?" I ask, unsure what CQ means.

CQ nods, sucking on her kiss. "Designing a life requires befriending Anxiety. Annoying, constricting anxiety becomes Leaping Anxiety—she gives you the energy to leap toward what you want, and Fierce Desire keeps you up there. Then you use healthy comforts and courage to help you glide and wiggle your way through Fear."

"You make it sound as if I have to live in a constant state of anxiety and fear."

"Well, don't you anyway?"

I stop in the middle of the road and consider the truth of her words. The weight of my fears presses on my shoulders. I deepen my breath and I ask myself, for the millionth time, What am I afraid of?

CQ hugs me to her side. "The poet Louise Bogan wrote, 'I cannot believe that the inscrutable universe turns on an axis of suffering; surely the strange beauty of the world must somewhere rest on pure joy!' Anxiety and Fear never go completely away, but they *will* lose their power over you. You *are* gaining enough experience to trust your courage and enough determination to surrender."

I try leaping, imagining myself as Twyla Tharp suspended in the air.

I stumble. CQ applauds anyway.

"You always have a choice. You can breathe, trust, and surrender or you can run on ego and away from fear. You've seen where that gets you."

Yes, I had very clearly seen where that got me. I leap again.

HOW WOULD I DESCRIBE MY LIFE RIGHT NOW? WHAT IS THE TRUTH, WITHOUT BLAME, SHAME, THEORY, OR PROJECTIONS INTO THE FUTURE? WHAT IS THE TRUTH OF MY LIFE RIGHT NOW?

Record only the facts, which can take a few tries. Here is an example: "I am in a business situation with two partners that feels bad to me. I don't want to go to work. I feel very frustrated trying to work with them. I feel very disappointed and sad that this hasn't worked out. I feel I'm spinning around in circles. My husband has noticed that I'm being a victim. I loved being in the store and learning this business before." As Robert Johnson and Jerry Ruhl write in *Contentment*, "Just state what is. . . . When you sincerely state what is in any given situation, a mysterious thing happens. 'What is' is made conscious, and you are then able to see the next 'what is.' You do that thing and ask yourself again, 'What is?' Then you do the next right thing. In this stepwise manner you can gradually get your life moving in a positive direction." This question is difficult. CQ takes on her pen shape and helps you tackle it. "We'll circle around, sneak up on your life. I know this is about as fun as balancing your checkbook while getting your legs waxed, but, hey, think how smooth and organized you'll feel afterward."

(continued on next page)

WHAT AM I GRATEFUL FOR? WHAT AM I NOT GRATEFUL FOR?
WHAT DO I FEEL THAT I SHOULD BE GRATEFUL FOR
BUT I CAN'T MUSTER UP THE JUICE?

Gratitude is a powerful, ancient way of coming into divine balance, but it cannot be forced and it cannot be sentimentalized. By naming the truth of your state of gratitude, you will then find what you are authentically grateful for.

WHAT ADVICE HAVE I BEEN GIVING LATELY?
AM I FOLLOWING THAT ADVICE FOR MYSELF?

If you can't recall ladling out advice lately, imagine what you would say to a friend who was living a life identical to yours. If possible, say what you have to say aloud. Then ask yourself,

WHAT PART OF THIS ADVICE AM I WILLING TO FOLLOW?

These are arduous questions. Give yourself a sensuous treat for even reading them. CQ adds, "I recommend coconut oil, African drum music, and lithe younger men. Works for me."

Kali, Spirals, and It Is What It Is

Patience, creativity, agility, and a fierce desire to see *Masterpiece Theater.* Self-nurturing and self-love as the ground of one's being. A more distinct portrait of what constituted CQ was emerging, an image of what I was stretching toward. And I couldn't forget her hawk-eyed compassion, the part of her that was so discomforting yet invigorating. Like the Hindu goddess Kali, who intrigued and frightened me as much as CQ did, she and the women I was meeting and interviewing were a "force within the universe that cuts through misconceptions. . . . On another level she [they] can be seen as a symbol of the fact that there is something larger going on in life that is not influenced by, nor does it yield to, the ways of humankind" as China Galland describes Kali in *The Bond Between Women.*

I had experienced a Kali–Comfort Queen moment with Marcie when she had bandied about the phrase "It is what it is," as she had been doing for many months. Because she often speaks in symbolic language, and because I like to pretend I know what everyone is talking about, I hadn't asked her before exactly what she meant. Instead, I tried to absorb it. Then one day we went for a hike up Lady of the Lake trail, an undulating passage ornately encrusted with moss, rolling through stands of pine, so utterly feminine and primeval that I half-expected to see a jeweled hand emerge from the lake at the end of the trail, offering an enchanted sword.

As we hiked, I ranted about my hurry-up-devour-the-world quality and how tired I was of being this way and how impossible it was to change. Marcie turned and said, "What if that is just the way you are?" In unison we cackled, "It is what it is." In that patch of woods, the sun falling on the juicy green moss, a spring trickling on either side, for one sweet instant I just was. I was me, full on, without my usual defenses of fantasy—faced with the truth about myself, I have two routine responses: it isn't as bad as I think, or tomorrow I will change. It was so enlivening—facing myself, feeling both compassion and "Really, that's me? How incredibly ugly." There was no place to hide, no excuses to make.

It is what it is.

Whack! Slice to the essence of the thing, right through the excuses, the psychobabble, the what-if's, and see the moment for what it is. Study it unflinchingly, nothing between you and it. Give up trading in certainties and fantasies.

Therapist and author Stephanie Dowrick writes about a long and difficult legal battle she was mired in for three years, about how she "gave up thinking, 'This must end because it should, because I need it to, because it makes no sense for it to continue, because it is hurting everyone involved.' Such thoughts came to seem unbearably hollow to me and I literally could not endure it when other people voiced any of those same sentiments. Oddly enough, I gained courage and regained resilience when I gave up wishing that life was other than it was; when I gave up wishing that events were other than they were; when I surrendered to the painful truth of what was."

In *Composing a Life,* Mary Catherine Bateson makes a brilliant point about the spiral nature of life, about accepting life as it is: "There has been the tendency to look ahead to some sort of utopia in which women will no longer be torn by the conflicting claims and desires that so often turn their pathways into zigzags or, at best, spirals. *And yet these very conflicting claims are affirmations of value* [italics mine]. It would be easier to live with a greater clarity of ambition, to follow goals that beckon toward a single upward progression. But perhaps what women have to offer in the world today, in which men and women both must learn to deal with new orders of complexity and rapid change, lies in the very rejection of forced choices: work or home, strength or vulnerability, caring or competition, trust or questioning. Truth may not be so simple."

Part of me knew on a cellular level what Stephanie and Mary Catherine meant. The other part of me thought that if change is not the point, I might as well curl up with 10 pounds of Sara Lee frosted brownies (frozen) and watch a Roller Derby marathon. Black-and-white is not only more comforting; it looks good on everybody.

"Change happens, only it grows, organically, ravishingly, from acceptance of the unfinished reality that is life." CQ's voice, accompanied by an odd buzzing, booms through my house. "Certainties and when-then fantasies are colossal energy-suckers. When you reject dualism, as Kali does, you free so much potential and energy."

As I go in search of CQ, I talk to the walls at large, not knowing where she'll turn up but pretty sure she'll hear me. "You want me to stop believing the voice which tells me that moving forward is the only point to life, that getting better is the only goal, and by the way, since I've never been able to *perfectly* accomplish anything, I must be a complete and abysmal failure at *everything*?" I laugh at the absurdity of what I've just said.

I find CQ in the backyard. She is standing in the middle of an enormous spiral. It emerges from the ground and rises to the tree line, about sixty feet high, and then fades off into the sky. The spiral is twisting up, then curling down, all the while making a high-tension buzz. She stands in a spiral, talking, as if this is the most normal thing in the world. For her, I guess it is. "I know that hurry-up-and-get-perfect voice all too well," she says. "He was my first husband. Let me tell you, that guy was one boring son of gun at parties. He spent the entire time straightening the cocktail napkins. The only way I ever got anywhere with that man was to stop fighting him. I would stand there, pretending to listen to his sermons." CQ motions me closer as she continues. "He hated that I didn't do exactly what he wanted when he wanted, so he left me for Martha Stewart." Her cackle echoes off the house.

"What is this?" I ask, feeling a little shaky. "Am I going too far out, losing touch with reality? Is this what happens when you follow your unfolding path?"

"This? This is the spiral of your life." CQ adopts a radio-announcer voice. "It resembles the ancient symbols of the ivy and the grapevine. The Celts recognized it as a symbol of rebirth and resurrection. Today we see the spiral in the DNA molecule, the basis of all life." She steps on the spiral, rides it up a bit, then down. "Life is a spiral. You keep visiting the same stuff over and over again, but each time you see it from a different perspective."

I walk closer, more fascinated now than alarmed. "A therapist once said to me the only way humans learn is to gain a little bit of informa-

73

tion and then go around again until you meet yourself, the self who was deprived or angry or hurt in the past, but this time you know a little bit more, you see a little bit more." I reach out my hand to touch the spiral. "She believes it isn't about getting better or conquering your problems; it is about seeing and accepting what you see."

"That's exactly it," CQ steps out of the spiral. It dwindles until it fits in the palm of her hand. "Accepting the spiral, building that idea into creating your life—that's yet another quality you need."

"What's another?"

CQ smiles at me. "You're always trying to get me to give you the answers. I can't. You have to find them for yourself." She pushes my hair off my forehead, and the spiral gives me a little jolt. "The most basic rule of spiritual evolution is that you have to discover things for yourself. If I tell you, it will slide off your back like a compliment. But I'm a soft touch and I adore you, so here's a clue: Freud."

As I watch CQ walk through the garden gate, the Freud clue reminds me of Nora Gallagher, whom I sidle up to at parties in the hope that some of her equanimity and spiritual depth will rub off on me. I had often turned to her book *Things Seen and Unseen* during my dark time. Nora and I had recently attended a birthday lunch for a dear friend, and we had each given her a book as a gift. The conversation turned to what we were reading. "I read an essay about Freud over Christmas," Nora said. "Freud said people keep thinking they can resolve things, and the truth of the matter is we cannot. There is very little we can resolve. Instead, the way to have a greater love of life and to become happier, or at least to become less neurotic, is to increase our capacity for conflict and to increase our capacity for complexity."

Alone in my yard, I lie down in the grass and watch the ants. They know exactly what their job is, exactly what they will do each day for the rest of their lives. "Complexity" and "ambiguity" are not words you use to describe ants.

I could be envious of these ants. . . . But aren't complexity and ambiguity incredibly more interesting?

HOW CAN I DANCE WITH MYSTERY IN THE DAYS AHEAD?

Thomas Moore writes in *The Care of the Soul* that the soul "insinuates, offers fleeting impressions, persuades more with desire than with reasonableness.... The soul's indications are many, but they are usually extremely subtle." There is no logical answer to this question. But ask it anyway and see what insinuates itself into your mind and heart.

WHERE AM I WALKING MY TALK THESE DAYS?
WHERE ARE MY OUTER ACTIONS AND UTTERANCES REFLECTING
MY INNER REALITY? HOW AM I LIVING AND INVESTING THROUGH
ACTION WHAT I'M FEELING AND HEARING INSIDE?

CQ puts her arm around your shoulder. "If you say no, you are not walking your talk, I challenge you to remember that nothing is black-and-white. There are always places where you *are* walking your talk and places where you *are not*. Hold my hand while you look. You don't have to *do* anything, just look."

FOR WHAT DO I NEED TO FORGIVE MYSELF?
IS THERE ANYONE ELSE I NEED TO FORGIVE?

It doesn't have to be big and it doesn't have to be whole, finished; it can be a keyhole you peer through for a moment, a softening of your heart for a split instance. Who are you afraid to forgive?

IF I LET MY BODY TALK, WHAT WOULD SHE SAY?
WHAT IS MY BODY TRYING TO TELL ME?

CQ strokes your arm. "Stop in this moment, my dear. Let your breath glide in and out, and ask your tender animal of a body what she is trying to tell you. She is on your side; she really is."

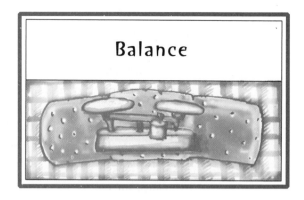

Balance

A woman goes to her doctor and says, "I'm exhausted." The doctor says, "You've got to take care of yourself, take some time for yourself." The woman slumps in her chair and sighs, "That's one more person I've got to take care of."

Years ago I taught a workshop at a large Canadian bank. The workshop was for middle managers, and the participants were all women. I was told that women were hired as middle managers because "they are always willing to go the extra mile, put in the extra hours, make it work." A few hours into the day-long workshop, one woman blurted out, "This feels like another 'should'; taking care of myself is just something else to put on my to-do list."

That's when I began to see signs of a balance backlash everywhere, signs that self-nurturing as a way to know yourself, or even as a way to take ten minutes to chill out, was turning into a "should" instead of an inspiration, a straitjacket of expectations.

Joan Borysenko describes a similar observation in *A Woman's Book of Life:* "Many books tout the benefits of taking more time for ourselves, and suggest that if we don't, we're psychologically or spiritually in the wrong. While it is crucial for women to take some time each day for themselves to recharge, it is often impossible to take very much. But perhaps we don't need very much. I know that even a few minutes of prayer or meditation rejuvenates me as does caring for my houseplants, walking through the garden, calling a friend, taking a walk, doing a little yoga, or reading a book. The problem is that many books suggest that I should be able to do all of those things most every day, scolding me if I don't. If I believed them I'd feel guilty for ignoring myself, a guilt which many women now experience." Borysenko compares the balanced woman to the Victorian psychic figure of the Angel in the House, "the perfect example of the feminine mystique—demure, self-sacrificing, caring more for the needs of others than her own, and deriving power by borrowing it from a man." We are not yet free of the Angel of the House; in fact, she has morphed into the "inner and outer voices that criticize the busy woman for being out of balance.... The perfect woman of Virginia Woolf's generation, and my mother's after hers, was supposed to have plenty of time for leisure, family, and friendship pursuits. The Angel's admonitions haven't changed over the years, only her clothing has. Now she wears the vestments of a kind of generic spirituality, and utters instructions on how to live a perfectly balanced life as a kind of Angelic Traditional Priestess. Her spiritual garb makes her gibes particularly sharp, since she pretends to hold the true keys to our happiness."

When we see balance as a "should" that we must attain the right way, we're just practicing another form of perfectionism. Balance doesn't mean you work 7.5 hours, exercise 20.3 minutes at a heart rate of 82 percent, then spend 2.4 quality hours with your children. Balance doesn't even mean you nurture yourself every day. This kind of balance is a misleading Band-Aid and is about as realistic as choosing Camelot as your vacation destination. We want to believe in this comforting fairy-tale formula, for at first it feels like a cool cloth pressed against our feverish foreheads. But when we try to live this prescription, we find that it is oppressive, and it misses the point entirely. It makes us anxious because it imposes a shape on our lives—what balance should be.

We've got it backwards—we are trying to fit ourselves into a generic picture of balance. Instead, we must first find out who we really are, then arrange the elements of our lives (while compromising with those we love), in order to create the life we are meant to have. That's divine balance. Creating a complex, meaningful life from our essence. It may, at times, look insanely busy, lumpy in one area, scant in another, but if we keep listening, what will emerge is the powerful, dynamic life that is truly ours.

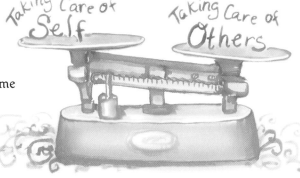

I mention compromising with those we love because all my listening and deciding for myself become almost moot when framed against my child's "Mommy, Mommy, play with me." As the mother of a small child, I find that the pace and life that are best for me are rarely the pace and life that are best for my child. As a mother, I have desperately wanted to believe there is a formula for harmony that would ensure I was giving my child enough. I have had to learn, in a continually messy and painful way, that there isn't. My child needs tons of attention and time from her parents. She does not like it that we work, that we travel for work, that we have work that we love passionately, and that sometimes we would rather work than be with her. My divine balance comes from working *and* being with Lilly. Lilly's balance comes from being with her mom and dad.

When faced with a child's needs or a religious calling like Nora Gallagher's or political dedication like Maria Harris's, our mass-produced ideal of balance is split down the middle, ripped ragged, and opened up for the larger energies to move through. This is yet another moment when our will bends before the will of the Other. Consider this for a moment: What if our attempts to do everything, to accomplish, to grasp at life, are *not* about proving we are good enough but are the insistent tugs of our guardian angel? "Over here, do this, hurry up, this is what you are supposed to be doing," she mutters. What if, somewhere in us, we are aware of what we are here to do but our mortal bodies can't quite keep up with our angel's agenda?

In the end, if we spend all our time listening or trying to become balanced, how boring! Devotion, action, and reality transmute us, create the tension and chaos that are indispensable to the creative process. We are aimed toward this by the question "What one thing could I do in the days ahead to become the person I most want to be?" Although as women we must fight our socialization to always put ourselves last, we must also be strong enough to surrender our vision, our drive, to Mystery, whether Mystery comes in the package of a very small child, the querulous skin of an elderly parent, or the luminous glow of the alarm clock dial summoning us to the day.

Yet another paradox appears: the only way we do this is by listening.

WHAT'S HAPPENING WITH MY OBSTACLES TO RELAXATION AND SELF-NURTURING NOW?

Look back at page 17. Have your obstacles shifted? Perhaps new ones have sprung up or you are feeling ready to deal with one in a more proactive fashion? Is there one modest step you could now take to eliminate one of these obstacles?

WHERE AM I MOST AFRAID OF BEING SELF-INDULGENT OR SELF-ABSORBED? IN THE LAST FEW WEEKS, WHEN HAVE I BEEN? WHEN SHOULD I HAVE BEEN?

Only by asking and listening will you know. CQ notes, "Remember, self-indulgent women don't ask; they shop."

WHAT SIMPLE ACTION DO I NEED TO REMEMBER, SOMETHING I HAVE DONE IN THE PAST THAT RELAXED ME, HELPED ME REGAIN MY SANITY AND PERSPECTIVE?

Putting music on while you work, taking a real lunch break, going for a walk with your family after dinner, doing half a yoga exercise tape, throwing five things away from the junk drawer, paying someone to clean your car or house, sitting down with a friend and brainstorming solutions to a pressing problem or stressful situation.

CQ chimes in, "Just in case you need a few more ideas, you could chant "Om" three times (even if you don't live on the West Coast), buy some bubbles and blow them at work (pun intended), sit by a fountain, sleep outside, or slurp tapioca pudding while watching a Katharine Hepburn movie."

Verve Talk

Comfort Queen Stories

Stories are sustenance, particularly stories of how women are creating their lives. Imagine a spacious living room lit by candles. Darkness, big trees, and an overgrown late-summer garden press comfortingly against the French windows. Picture a ring of fluffy couches, languorous chaises, and well-padded rocking chairs. In these chairs sit women of all ages, colors, and sizes. They are sitting in silence together, speaking occasionally, offering a feast of their spirit to each other.

Christine speaks up from her sprawled position on a chaise. "After my father died a little over a year ago, my three sisters and I sat down with my seventy-year-old mother, who is five feet one and has always been quite timid and shy, to talk to her about moving in with one of us. She had lived almost her whole life in the suburbs, and now here she was on forty acres in the middle of nowhere. We calmly explained that this was too much for her to manage. The house had only wood heat! She listened and seemed to agree with us. The very next week she called and left a giddy message on my phone. 'I bought a tractor,' she said, with an almost audible smile. In the year since that purchase, my mother has become a much stronger and more opinionated woman than I ever thought possible. She has completely blossomed into living the life she always wanted. And she loves her tractor."

Another voice, Sarah, speaks up low but firm: "I have been thinking a lot about what it means to be courageous and to become a better person, and how that is one way to frame creating your life. I was sexually abused as a child and also as an adult, so being in my body has never been easy for me. Six months ago, I decided to go into the center of what I am afraid of. I hired a yoga teacher to come to my house twice a week. This is an enormous indulgence for someone with my income. He always comes at the same time of day, yet I never know which day he will show up. So five days a week I do my yoga practice. Most days it is uncomfortable and I want out. Many days I have cried and my whole body has shaken. But I am determined that one day I will be in my body without terror. Now it has been more than a month since I cried during yoga, and today my body did things it has never done. It is the beginning of a freedom I have never known. Being willing to go into my discomfort is changing my life."

"I had a body moment like that recently, too." Nicole speaks above the creaking of her rocking chair. "I was hustling around on campus, thinking about the computer program that was due, the calculus exam I had to write, my full-time job, and a disaster I had just overcome—very gracefully, I might add—and from nowhere my inner critic starts in on me about my weight. This time I didn't take it. I found myself saying to her, "Look, I know I need to lose weight, but I've got a lot on my plate right now, so please stop nagging me. I go to the gym almost every day, I do my yoga, you are not doing anything helpful, and I'm too busy to spend time listening to you. *Stop!* In the space after I declared 'Stop,' in that moment, I found myself present; instead of being with what didn't exist—my imaginary perfect body. Instead of worrying about all the things I can't change. For a moment I was able to be proud of everything that was right about my life."

Several voices murmur, "Sounds delicious" and "You go, girl."

"This was a turning point for me." Sheila arranges herself more comfortably, takes a breath, goes on. "At thirty-five, I was preparing to marry a wonderful man. It was a first marriage for both of us. I still considered myself the baby of the family. During trips home for the holidays, I would immediately click back into the 'child' role once I crossed my parents' threshold. I would allow everything to continue between my parents—the way we communicate, for example—as if I was still nine. But then came the announcement of my marriage. My parents cheerfully agreed to pay for the wedding as their gift to us. But then they asked me to come to them at each stage of the plans and ask for a check. It quickly became clear to my fiancé that

gaining control by using money was an old, old pattern in our family. After a lot of conversation, tears, and therapy, I went to my parents, thanked them for their offer, and told them we had decided to postpone the wedding until we could pay for it ourselves. The look on my parents' faces—they were shocked. They never expected this. It was this step that brought me to adulthood not only in my parents' eyes but in my own as well. My husband later told me he could not have married the person who existed before I took that step. He knew I had the potential to be my own person, but until that moment he didn't know if I had the strength to take that step. The funniest thing was my father wrote me a check that night for the entire amount and agreed not to stand in the way of any of our plans."

"Your wedding story reminds me of a turning point in my life, more than thirty-five years ago," said Diana, smiling gently as she remembered. "This story is a thank-you to a childhood mentor whom I have not yet had a chance to thank. This is because I did not realize a thank-you was in order until recently. My husband and I were having a discussion over breakfast about the silent pecking order that exists at work. My husband made the comment that if those perceived to be on top at work made a mistake, it was brushed aside and forgotten. However, if a poor soul who was perceived to be less important made a mistake, he or she became the center of a dartboard. Then my husband said what struck me most: 'In order for an inconsequential person to break out of her lowly place, it really helps if one of the respected and highly regarded people reaches down to mentor her.' I transferred from my parochial school to a public high school in ninth grade. I knew no one. The culture at the parochial school had been very strict and stifling, so I stuck out like I was wearing a habit at my new school. You could actually talk in the hallways. At Catholic school, we had to stand up and push in our chairs before answering a question. The kids in my biology class got a kick out of that one on my first day. I had not been allowed to shave my legs yet. Just imagine what dark hair squished under panty hose looked like. I had not been allowed to wear a bra . . . just a T-shirt. Having to undress in front of the girls to take a public shower after gym brought all this to light. Needless to say, I dreaded going to school. I was teased a lot. I was not making friends. Then along came Nancy. You can pick out the elite circle of kids in any grade, and Nancy was the queen. She was tall and shapely, with bright auburn hair set off by beautiful green eyes. She was so expressive and sure of herself. She wore the neatest clothes and was a modern jazz dancer. The other girls were beautiful and special in their own ways, too, but Nancy was the queen. She *saw* me. She felt for me. She befriended me. She helped me pick out a pattern for a stylish dress and the material to make it. I had such a hard time knowing what I liked or didn't like. I didn't have any opinions at all. Trying to pick out material was so difficult for me, it made me wonder why. This little incident triggered my search for myself. Nancy sewed the stylish new dress for me, the frump. I still remember the colors—bright yellow on top with a very short black-and-white houndstooth skirt. I don't think her friends understood why she was helping me. We went to Mexico together for six weeks as part of a student Spanish program where she guided and guarded me in that real-life place far from home. I am just now realizing how much of a difference she made in my self-image and in my life to follow. Her acceptance and gracious mentoring were angelic, validating me as a viable person. Wouldn't it be grand to do the same for those around us who have been silently classified as the untouchables?"

Silence and the sputtering of candles take over the room, as each woman revisits her role in adolescence.

"I took charge of my life a few months ago," said Nina. "When I started thinking about creating my life, I discovered I wanted to work less. I wanted more time with my kids, more time to move my body, to work with my dreams, to have an inner life, even more time to do the dishes. But there didn't seem to be any way because our budget was so tight. Then one day my youngest, who is nine, said, "Can't you just sit still and talk to me? I have a problem." Here I was, going ninety miles an hour, not giving her the attention she needed. That was it. That night I started taking control of our financial life. I found ways to cut five hundred dollars from our budget. I canceled the cable service, I refinanced the house, switched our car insurance to a cheaper company, and started seeing spending *money* as spending my *time*. Within a month, I was able to cut my work back a day and a half each week. I have refused to fill that time with busywork. It is time for me or the kids, not for cleaning, running errands, or anything unimportant. Whenever I start to let unimportant things crowd in, I remember I couldn't have done it before because I would have been at work. Believing that I could create what I wanted and realizing it was up to me to make it happen, that was the shift I needed."

What is your story of creating your life?

Where is your tractor?

WHAT DO I WANT TO CREATE AND BRING FORTH FROM MYSELF IN THE
COMING DAYS? WHAT IS THE MOST VITAL THING FOR ME TO INITIATE?

We are probably *not* talking about big projects. Here are some examples from
women's lives: gathering material for an altar, calling the high school to see about
being a mentor to a young girl, taking my daughter on an overnight hike, dancing a
dream, setting up a weekly meditation session at church, creating a monthly medi-
ated clear-the-air session with my team at work.

WHAT IS THE FIRST STITCH OF HANDIWORK
I NEED TO MAKE THIS CREATION A REALITY?

What is the first step? Perhaps it is going through drawers and old boxes to find significant objects for my altar, visiting the school to meet girls and see if I click with
anyone, putting an ad in the church bulletin, calling the county mediation program
to see if someone can help me.

IF I COULD TAKE A *SNAPSHOT OF THE HEART* FROM THE LAST FEW DAYS,
A TENDER, RAVISHING MOMENT THAT I WANT TO HOLD CLOSE AND
REMEMBER, WHAT WOULD I CHOOSE?

A child's silhouette framed in sunlight, your cat writhing in pleasure on the
stone steps, a moment of connection and belonging
between you and a friend.

WHAT IS THE CYNIC OR CRITIC SAYING ABOUT THESE QUESTIONS?
WHAT FEARS ARE FLOATING TO THE SURFACE?

No judgment, just awareness. "Awareness, my dear, is your precious elixir," CQ gently reminds you.

Choosing and Mindful Listening

I wake to a spicy, earthy smell wafting through our bedroom. I practice my morning devotional of studying my daughter's and husband's slumbering profiles, their tender faces framed by tousled blankets. I say a brief prayer for guidance before padding upstairs in my slippers. CQ is in the kitchen, cooking. "Good morning. Here's your tea."

Instead of her usual crown, CQ is wearing a turban and a carrot-colored apron, and she's stirring a bubbling concoction with her scepter. "I had to get here early when I realized we haven't talked about choosing yet. We still have so much to cover, but this can't wait. Choosing is the axis on which creating your life turns. Without choosing, there is no creation. Your life depends on the choices you make, how you approach the smorgasbord. I don't see women choosing. Too often I see them either trying to do everything or believing they can do nothing." CQ chops chilies and mangoes and adds them to the soup. "Choosing mindfully is the beginning of making friends with Anxiety and Fear."

"What do you mean?"

"You may think you'll avoid a rendezvous with Anxiety and Fear by not choosing. But what happens is when you don't choose, Anxiety and Fear get everything in your life all sticky. But when you commit to something, declare what you want, they get right in your face. Then you can use them like matching his and her pitchers of gogo juice to reenergize your commitment to being fully alive."

"So if I don't choose, I have free-floating anxiety and terminal fear. If I choose, then I can make them work for me."

"Exactly." CQ busies herself with the soup and I thoughtfully sip my tea. The taste of my tea brings me back to Stacey's luncheon. Every year, Stacey gathers a large group of women together for conversation, tea, and quiche, and to hear a speaker on women's inner lives. This year I shared a table with four women, two of whom I knew slightly. We dived into a conversation about how many things we want to do and don't have time for. One woman commented, "I feel like so many wonderful waves come my way. Waves I really want to take. But I can't. I have to dive deep under the wave, let it break over my head." She put her hand on her chest. "That causes me a tremendous amount of real sorrow. Those waves are interesting and I want to take them all." We nodded as we pictured our own waves: the people, groups, causes, projects, lectures, paintings, books, and music we would each love to engage with but can't. As I thought about it, my friend Kim's gentle face came to mind. One of the most talented and giving women I know, she has a difficult time knowing what she has the time and energy for. After two years of struggling with full-time volunteer work at her children's school, she had extracted herself, finally said, "No more." Yet she was already tempted to say yes to new commitments. "I have to keep reminding myself that my plate is already full," she says. "I can't replace my volunteer work with something else. But there is this little voice in my head that whispers, 'What about this class? What about this project?' It is so hard to say no *because I want to do everything.*"

CQ brings me back to the present: "You are ignoring the fact that you each have a limited amount of energy, time, and money to create a life with, and because you aren't clonable—although that may soon change—you have to choose. You've got to be willing to make the simple and arduous, sometimes austere and painful choices to stay true to the life unfolding within you. Pass the salt." CQ adds salt, tastes the soup, frowns, then reaches for a sooty, furrowed, tuberous thing, and adds a generous shaving of it to the soup. I shudder when she puts the root down and it moves a little on its own.

"CQ, I have learned to say no to the things I *do* want to do but can't. But I get flack from other people because so often I say, "I can't.""

"Try saying, 'I choose not to.' That will piss them off even more." She spots me rolling my eyes. "What, that doesn't sound like good advice? When you say 'I choose not to,' you take the reins. You are creating your life, instead of guilt or another of my ex-husbands, Mr. Should."

I knew she was right (she always is). Choosing is the fulcrum on which our lives turn. Especially as we reach middle age, we are aware, sometimes savagely, of how each week that passes is another week we are closer or further away from our truth. Then why are we so easily distracted? Because we love relationships and we don't want to say no to the people we love. Because our feminine conditioning to put ourselves last cannot be escaped in one or two generations. Because, as Elizabeth Lesser puts it in *The New American Spirituality,* "Life in reality involves real sacrifice. When you find what you really love, whether it's a person, a job, or a place, you must give up something as well. . . . [yet] We cannot sacrifice something that we have not yet made our own." In other words, choosing means knowing ourselves well enough and being strong enough to claim our yearnings while recognizing that we don't always get what we yearn for.

"Women have been torn between doing and loving for aeons. But it isn't an either-or. It's a continuum." CQ extracts a very long noodle from the soup and stretches it along the counter. "You don't have to choose between here and here." She slices off the ends of the noodle with our biggest knife. "You keep moving along the length. Becoming whole, reaching that place of 'It is what it is,' comes through holding the tension of wanting to spend more time on your inner life *and* wanting to be successful in the world, or wanting to exercise *and* wanting to take a nap. You say, 'I love my daughter and I love my work. What am I supposed to do? I can't be in two places at once.' Keep bringing your awareness to the opposites—how do I keep them both in my life? Right now, so many women are trying to hold on by being hyperorganized. You need organization and wildness, to hold the value of both. Crack open your idea of balance and let something unexpected bloom."

"A friend said to me that she had stopped trying to find the spot where she would no longer feel pulled between her beloved work and her two children. She just started being with both feelings, sitting on the couch and crying, but not saying anymore, 'When this happens, things will be easier.' This must be what Bateson is getting at; it's another aspect of the spiral."

CQ nods in agreement. "Now you're getting it." She sucks the noodle between her teeth and swallows. "It's Freud's point, too."

"Any Comfort Queen tricks you can teach me that might help?" I lean toward her.

CQ tilts her turban rakishly, eyes twinkling. "I said I couldn't tell you the answers but I never said I couldn't give you the questions."

WHAT IS ONE ISSUE I'M FEELING TWO CONTRADICTORY IMPULSES ABOUT?

Rose says, "I create my life by knowing when I'm in internal conflict, when I want two opposing things at the same time, and giving myself space to sit with that uncomfortable ambivalence or conflict." I want to feel better and I want to eat chocolate, but sugar doesn't make me feel good. Jeanie wants to write her grant proposal and she wants to goof off with her boyfriend. Diane needs the security of a regular paycheck but she doesn't like her boring job. These issues, large and small, are the stuff of our life, every day, now and forever. What is *one* issue in your life right now?

WHAT DO THE DIFFERENT VOICES INSIDE ME HAVE TO SAY ABOUT THIS PUSH-PULL?

Avoid a struggle by telling yourself (or hearing CQ tell you), "There is no right way." Gather their opinions, and let every part of you be heard, without rushing to judgment.

WHAT GREATER WHOLE COULD EMBRACE BOTH MY DESIRES?

This is a huge question. It may require time to blossom. You may need to sit with Ms. Anxiety, hold the tension of the opposites. "Beseech the goddesses for guidance, ask them to suggest a new way of seeing these rival desires," CQ advises. "But you must let yourself believe, even if just for a nanosecond, that some completely new way of approaching this area of your life *could* emerge. The gods require faith."

Mindful Listening

You create your life anew each day. As the Buddhist monk Thich Nhat Hanh writes, "Every morning, when we wake up, we have twenty-four brand-new hours to live. What a precious gift! We have the capacity to live in a way that these twenty-four hours will bring peace, joy, and happiness to ourselves and others." One of the ways we do that is to wake up to our right to choose, over and over again, and to do so with loving care. Visionary writer and teacher Elia Wise expands this idea in *Letter to Earth:* "To discover and realize your powers and your nature as a Universal Being meet the challenges of the moment honestly with choices that reflect the values and understanding you truly feel. By this action you will propel yourself toward enlightenment. It does not matter if what you feel to be your highest value turns out to be just another socially programmed idea or even a prideful, self-righteous notion. What matters is that you are willing *to live it, to invest yourself in it,* and to find out what it has to reveal to you about yourself and the nature of All That Is" (italics mine). When I get confused about choosing, I remember I don't have to be right, I only have to try with all my energy and integrity to be *true* to what I hear *in the moment.*

Yet using my energy and integrity to make these choices is not easy. The events of my life and my reaction to them are usually all mashed together. I don't know what to choose because I don't know what I'm feeling, I don't have enough breathing room. When we moan, "There is never enough time," it is partly because of this emotional mashing. Our inner world cannot keep up with our actions. We have no time to deliberate, collect ourselves, ruminate, "Is what is being asked of me in line with my values? Does it expand my life or tread all over me? Does it support who I am and who I am becoming?" Mindful listening pries apart our feelings and our actions so that a little bit of fresh air can squeeze in between an event and our response to it. By practicing this, we create a way to choose more consciously (for we will choose, consciously or not). Time is not measured by clocks. Time is measured by our perceptions. If we perceive everything to be one frantic rush, then it is. If we perceive ourselves able to stop, inquire, choose, reframe, then time slows down and our soul has time to catch up. (Huff, huff, here I come!) If we perceive ourselves free to choose, to create our lives, then often we are.

As women, we especially need this air space because our cultural conditioning has so cruelly twisted our love of relationships into a loss of self. Too often we are frantically looking outside of ourselves, asking, "What does he need? How about her? What does that person over there think of me? Am I enough?" We keep moving faster, trying to please, fill, perform, excel, *prove.*

This will only stop when *we* stop and make room for receptivity.

Be willing to receive guidance without demanding that it guide you in only the direction you are comfortable going. Be willing to hang out in the void without knowing. Don't move until you honestly stop to listen. When nothing is going your way, stop pushing and listen. "And this receptive nature must be married to intention and action," CQ says as she circles my desk in the form of an enormous lazy butterfly.

My eyes follow her as she flaps. "What are you getting at?" I ask.

"Sometimes you fish, sometimes you cut bait. The will is a powerful thing. The woman who knows when to use her will and when to put it away, creates the life she is meant to have," CQ the butterfly answers, wagging her antenna.

It is basic yet so hard to verbalize because it is in the void that we must wait. When we get overly fixated on doing or caring for others to prove our worth, we cut ourselves off from our mysterious source of being. We *have* to start in the goalless place and wait there, hushing and holding, until gradually the unfolding of our next step is revealed.

Helen Luke wrote in *The Way of Woman,* "If we can rediscover in ourselves the hidden beauty of this receptive devotion, if we can learn how to be still without inaction, how to further life without willed purpose, how to serve without demanding prestige, and how to nourish without domination: then we shall be women again out of whose earth the light may shine." Opening to what life is bringing and then working with that opening is how we let the inside shape the outside.

Simple, painstaking, and utterly foreign to how most of our world operates.

WHAT SWEET WORDS OF ENCOURAGEMENT DO I NEED
TO HOLD IN MY HEART AND HEAD IN THE COMING DAYS?

Pinpoint a discomfort or stress. Talk to yourself the way you would a child or a beloved pet. CQ adds, "Get specific about what you want to hear in your head. What will sustain you instead of deplete you?" Belleruth repeats to herself, "I welcome the daily perception of divine assistance all around me, guiding me to my true self and its joyful expression." Use this or ask CQ to inspire one that fits your life.

WHAT ONE PERSON HAVEN'T I BEEN FEELING
COMPLETELY COMFORTABLE WITH?

Whoever comes into your mind first is perfect.

WHAT DO I KNOW IN MY GUT IS NEEDED TO BRING THIS RELATIONSHIP
INTO A MORE HONEST AND BALANCED PLACE?

A small, heartfelt, honest action.

HOW CAN I CHERISH AND ENCHANT MY SWEET SELF?

ENTERTAINMENT: An evening of *Masterpiece Theater*, a tea party with girlfriends, a Saturday morning ignoring responsibilities and reading an appetizing mystery . . .

More Mindful Listening

This is how you practice mindful listening:

STOP. BE STILL.

With a little practice, you can do this quickly. I imagine a line running down my spine and another line running through my belly button. I sense where the two intersect and focus my attention there, breathing slowly and deeply. Three breaths, about thirty seconds to one minute, will center me—unless, of course, Lilly is whining like an Alaskan mosquito boring into my ear. There are thousands of such ancient stilling practices. Finding one that fits you is not the issue, overcoming your resistance to quieting down is. Use your will to quiet down; then you can release your will and listen.

ASK YOURSELF A QUESTION.

By now it has become abundantly clear that I am slightly obsessed with questions. You can also use a word, like "peace," "well-being," "center," or "love." I am not trying to replace the sacred mantras from great spiritual teachers. Instead, I'm trying to use the ancient practice of going within to foster a deeper, stronger sense of self. As Carol Flinders declares in *At the Root of This Longing,* "If a woman knows who she is, she cannot be drawn into an abusive relationship or manipulated by corporate media or prevented from playing an active role in politics that her country's laws entitle her to. She is quite simply immune to exploitation of any kind." That's what we're after.

CONSIDER.

After you look inside yourself and see what you need, you look outside yourself and see what others need, and you *bring the two together.* Two hands clapping. Sometimes you get what you want, sometimes your child or partner or boss does, and sometimes you both get a little of what you need. There is no resolution, only process. By knowing what we want and need, we paradoxically are able to give it up with less resentment, to more honestly give and serve others. As Shann says in *Independent Women* by Debra Sands Miller, "We move the locus of authority from the outside to the inside. And then follow it."

IMAGINE THIS:

You are feeling rushed and frantic because your parents are arriving in an hour, your child needs to be picked up from one birthday party and dropped at another. You haven't bought the fish for dinner yet. You most definitely haven't had time to tend your inner life lately. You have to pee. You go to the bathroom, shut the door, relax on your throne, close your eyes, breathe in and out—slowly now, that's right, I can do this. Okay, body, there now, "How can I flow with this day and be present to it?" What response creeps, pops, slithers, sings, whispers its way into your consciousness? Perhaps it is a memory of skiing, or perhaps your shoulders let go and you hear that you need to linger at the birthday party, connect with your child and her world, even if it means being late for your parents' arrival or having to go out later to buy the fish. Perhaps you experience an "ah," a letting-go of control, an opening to what will come. Or maybe you remember you have to buy carrots and onions after you buy the fish. Hey, that's important, too.

When do you do this check-in? When you are:
- Off-kilter
- Beset by urgency
- Worried
- Faced with a choice
- Overly focused on what others think of you
- Feeling not good enough
- In pain
- Depressed, blue
- On pins and needles, can't sit still, can't do inner work
- Reaching for shadow comfort (more about shadow comfort soon)
- Making love to your time monsters (and more about these critters, too)
- Sounding like Minnie Mouse: high, breathless, and fast
- Neglecting your dreams, body, writing, painting

- Hungry or thirsty
- Bruised, weary, hurt, or angry
- Full of an unnamable yearning, restless
- Full of energy and hope
- Wanting to make self-nurturing the ground of your being
- Abounding with verve
- When your prompt reminds you to do it (more about prompts in a moment)

"The moment you are in contains all that you need to master, all your lessons, all your opportunities—if you will listen to it and expand with it." I find myself in the kitchen and CQ is handing me a bowl of soup. "The gurus and sages are right. It really is all inside you. Let that cool off before you taste it."

I inhale the aroma of the soup. I had taught this method of check-in for years and yet how little I had practiced it! How long would I stick with it this time?

"Remember, you have more fierce desire now. You want it more. It also helps to have a prompt." CQ ladles herself soup and sits down next to me at the kitchen bar. "The Buddhists have a mindfulness bell. You can use your computer calendar to remind you. Bill Gates probably didn't imagine such a use when he talked about a computer on every desk in America, but then, he's never met the subversive wiles of a Comfort Queen." CQ grins slyly.

I decide to ask Chris to program my desktop pop-up program to beep six times a day, every two hours, to remind me to check in with myself. Chris gets inspired to try this and he uses his father's watch, which has an old-fashioned buzzing alarm. Amy chose a sound she hears regularly—the bells from the Santa Barbara mission. Shelly adapted a practice her dentist taught her for releasing her jaw. She scattered small stickers throughout her life, slightly out of her main line of vision—in the medicine chest, on the closet door, in the car visor, on the front door slightly above where she usually gazes. When she sees a sticker, she takes a deep, slow breath and asks herself a question.

Devon checks in with herself when her son, daughter, or partner yells for her from another room. "'Mommy, I'm hungry' is my special prompt," she says. "'Mommy, I need you to wipe my bottom,' however, doesn't usually give me time to pause." When Randi's cat meows, she's reminded to check in with herself.

Writer and therapist Gunilla Norris talks about her practice on her audiotape *Being Home.* She hangs a clothespin on a string in a doorway. Every time it nudges her, she stops, breathes, and repeats a word to herself, like "Peace." I've done this by hanging sachets in doorways I don't walk through constantly. Otherwise it becomes maddening–*bonk, bonk*–instead of centering. You could also try placing a few brightly colored Post-It notes with questions throughout your home.

What questions can you ask yourself? Some of the questions on the Living the Questions pages translate to this practice. The questions below work well too:

- ✴ What do I need right now?
- ✴ What does my body need right now?
- ✴ What does my spirit need right now?
- ✴ What am I not paying attention to? What am I ignoring?
- ✴ Am I being true to myself in this moment?
- ✴ Is this how I choose to spend my time? (Good to ask before you make a commitment or decision.)
- ✴ Is there something else I would rather be doing? (Good to ask when you are bored or restless.)
- ✴ What's most important to me right now?
- ✴ What is Divine Intelligence asking me to do?
- ✴ What do I need to do to be fully alive in this moment?
- ✴ How can I nurture myself today? (Great to ask in the early morning before getting out of bed.)
- ✴ What am I getting out of being so busy/frantic/overwhelmed? (Stop and ask yourself this in the moment of feeling crazy.)
- ✴ If I don't do this and it doesn't get done, will it matter?
- ✴ What do I yearn for right now?
- ✴ Does this support my life's intentions?

Make up your own questions. These aren't magic. Ask yourself: What question would help me listen to my wisdom? What would help me listen to Mystery? weave the threads of my life together? become whole?

Our questioning, over time, can loosen the duality of our lives. Our sense of being separated from the world decreases, bringing us closer to others because we are becoming more aware and accepting of ourselves. From this vantage point, time stops being something that runs our lives and starts being something we are in. Dwelling in.

Breathing in. Being.

And this wondrous state of affairs lasts for seconds at a time.

"Taste the soup now." CQ nudges me. I sip the swirling, steamy infusion. I get weepy with elation, my imagination pops with tangos and gospel songs, retreats into the redwoods, long soaks in sacred hot springs, pilgrimages to distant holy shelters, the cry of a hawk, and a slow walk around the block.

"Creators need lots of breaks. Don't ever forget that."

My brain stops whirring and my mouth takes over as I worshipfully sip.

Living the Questions

18

WHAT IS HAPPENING WITH MY STRESS POINTS AND/OR DISCOMFORTS?
WHAT COULD I DO TO RELIEVE ONE INSTANCE OF STRESS IN MY LIFE?
WHAT AM I TELLING MYSELF ABOUT HOW POSSIBLE THIS IS?

CQ nudges in: "I can just see you saying, 'It's impossible to not visit my mother, finish the project, buy the birthday present.' When you talk that way, you make a box of dingy, hobbling beliefs that cut off your vision. What *is* possible? Ask your sweet self that instead!"

WHO COULD I ASK FOR ONE SMALL,
SUMPTUOUS ACT OF SUPPORT TO EASE MY LIFE?

The angels, human and divine, need to be asked before they can help.

HOW CAN I ALLOW SILENCE INTO MY LIFE?

Focus on the word "allow."

AM I SEEING ANY SIGNS THAT I AM OUT OF BALANCE
OR HEADED FOR TROUBLE?

Look back at page 17 and check the list you made. Sometimes it is very obvious. Hell, yes, I'm out of balance. Sometimes it is more subtle, often because we are so sure being out of balance is normal. What have you been complaining about lately? And just what are your expectations of balance—are you still operating on balance as perfection instead of divine balance?

Auntie Goals

Ms. Insight
Ms. Yearning
Ms. Intention

Last January, I met with my friends Anna, Sandy, and Mary. We had chosen this day to set our goals for the coming year. Here were four bright, accomplished, spiritually aware women, ranging in age from thirty-six to fifty-one. That morning, not one of us was able to set a goal we felt truly passionate about. Between us we had read most of the goal-setting and visualization books and even brought an armload of them with us. Yet nothing fit, nothing felt right. We were tired of visualizing our ideal life, and we were equally tired of linear goals. We were caught somewhere between *Simple Abundance* and *The Seven Habits of Highly Effective People*. We left without setting one goal for the coming year.

Now I see we couldn't write a mission statement or name our goals or visualize our ideal day because we were imposing a shape on our lives from the outside, forcing ourselves into a pre-fab mold, instead of observing the shape our lives had already taken and then finding methods to gently work on the lumps and uneven places where our actions and thoughts weren't supporting this evolving shape.

We were mired in the old ways of getting things done: decide what we wanted and will it to happen, no matter what input we got to the contrary; put our heads down and ignore what wasn't working about our lives; or lapse into despair and overwhelm. None of these worked, none helped the larger energies to work through us.

"You love goals." Ms. Comfort Queen appears and begins taking the large number of goal books I own off my shelves. "You love New Age books which tell you that if you visualize your ideal life you'll get it. But they never work because you are creating from your mind instead of using your mind to help your soul. Goals are fixed, rigid. If you don't follow your inner voice, you may end up at a place you thought you wanted to be but no longer really do. You've been using goals, visualizations, and those little wish collages to tell the invisible forces what to do. You have to find a way to use these tools to *serve* your unfolding path." CQ heads toward the backyard. "I'm going to build a little fire and roast some marshmallows."

I tag along. "Okay, if I agree with you—and I'm not sure I do—then how do I follow my unfolding path without being passive? One minute I see what you and these other women are getting at, this listening and waiting business, and the next minute I'm sure you are wrong, that I need to push with everything I've got to make the most of myself while I'm still young(ish). Then I think, 'What kind of life is that?' Or I think about the women I've met in my workshops, the ones who had blackouts from stress or bad car accidents from rushing, and I think, Stop!"

"You need to give that willful side of yours a little breathing room. Don't count her out completely." Out in the yard, CQ makes a nice bonfire out of my goal books and toasts a marshmallow to perfection. "You have to control things, at least a little, that's who you are." I make an incredulous face at her words. "Who, me?"

CQ makes a face back, one that can best be described as a 3-D Kali-Gargoyle gross-out. I lurch back in horror. "Don't write about the Divine, the larger energies, the help that is available, as if almost everyone you know doesn't have a wee little problem with control. You teach yourself how to let go, but you leave some room for running the show, too. You've got to have both."

The Comfort Queen gives me a knowing smile and I have to laugh. She's right. I could never give up my controlling nature completely, at least not sober.

"I need a noncontrolling way to control my life."

"What you need, my dear, is the Auntie goals. Ms. Insight, Ms. Yearning, and Ms. Intention. These gals are wily provocateurs who share a rather anti-attitude toward traditional goals. These three sisters embrace crooked thinking, thrive on interruptions, relish the reality that life is a spiral, and fight to help women experience the passionate, multitude-of-interests life most of us are made for. The Aunties are Comfort Queen support staff. They help us remind women that goals and determination are to be handled gingerly, laced with a bit of unbridled lust. They eat paradox and bagels at teatime, wear Eau de Mystery perfume, and their favorite weekend adventure is setting out in a convertible with no destination." CQ imports a velvety lavender chaise to my backyard and reclines, sipping a piña colada. I raise an eyebrow at her cocktail consumption in the middle of the day.

She raises hers back. "Stop being such a Puritan. It's a virgin, anyway. I had a craving for coconuts."

"Exactly what is that crooked thinking?"

"Do you remember the play I quoted before, *Snake Talk* by Naomi Newman? She describes crooked thinking to a tee: 'Nothing natural or interesting grows in a straight line. As a matter of fact, it is the quickest way to the wrong place. And don't pretend you know where you are going. Because if you know where you are going, that means you've been there, and you are going to end up exactly where you came from.' Crooked thinking is jazz, baby, jazz."

Now where did I put that Covey planner and my prescription for Xanax? I'm more than skeptical, I'm having an anxiety attack. I ask her, "How exactly would I apply crooked thinking to my everyday *life*? How does it fit with this idea of shaping my life or remembering my sister-in-law's birthday? These Aunties sound dangerous."

"Stop trying to get from point A to point B in a straight line or in the shortest possible time," CQ comforts me. "Sometimes meandering is not only good, it's necessary. With too much linearity you cut the larger energies off at the knees, as well as any interesting encounters with handsome Tibetan strangers. You use what shows up, recycle what you can, occasionally take the long route. Another thing, which you are so good at preaching and not so good at living: stop assuming there is one right answer. A linear plan is sometimes very useful if you add, 'How would I get there if I had to walk a crooked path?' or 'How would I get there if I didn't have a clue where I wanted to get to?' or 'What would I see if I turned this plan upside down?' Listen to all the voices inside you. You are, after all, already listening to me. What's a few more? Invite interruptions."

The mere mention of interruptions sets my teeth on edge. I go inside to make myself some tea. If there was one central problem in creating my life, it was interruptions. Working at home with a young daughter for the last five years had raised the bar on interruptions to a dizzyingly new height. During the time I tried to write this section, I wiped Lilly's tears away three times, gave instructions to the baby-sitter when she arrived, made a picnic lunch, and I'm too exhausted to name everything else. I knew part of it was my boundaries, learning to delegate to people I hired, and the location of my office (next door to Lilly's room), but a huge part of it was *life*.

I put the kettle on and lean against the kitchen counter. When would my life get any easier?

CQ's coconut breath tickles my ear. "Never. Honey, you know it doesn't get easier. When it does, you don't like it. It is divine to be engaged with life. The Aunties will tell you to make use of these interruptions. Stop fighting them off and start asking them a few of your questions, see what you can learn from them. It is in fighting that you hurt yourself. Open your arms and welcome them."

I thought about what Jennifer Freed had said to me as we sat at her kitchen table. We were interrupted at least ten times by my daughter, her stepdaughter, and her partner. "Imagine you are taking a bus," she said. "The bus gets delayed and you're at a bus stop with somebody you've never met who ends up introducing you to someone who you end up having an incredible friendship with, a friendship that changes your life. If you pay attention, that's how our lives really go. Instead of being so angry when we don't get the bus on time, use that moment to reflect on why you have been stopped here. Don't take the interruption as proof that you shouldn't go or that you're failing. It's all a process. *Some* of these interruptions have secret guides within them. Learning to listen to those interruptions is vital. They are always there. I used to lock my keys in my car a lot. I would get furious. Then I started noticing that I always locked my keys in my car when I was angry. So every time I did it, it would slow me down, I'd revisit my day and ask, "Now, what was all the hurry and anger about?" It made me stop and check in. The conveyor belt we get on doesn't allow for this, so that's what interruptions do. It's all in how you incorporate the interruption."

I decide it is time for an interruption in the form of a nap. CQ tucks me in.

Living the Questions

19

WHAT DO I LIKE AND DISLIKE ABOUT MY MORNINGS?

Starting tomorrow, observe how you begin your day. What do you think about first thing? How do you greet the day? Set a watch, portable alarm, or your computer to go off every hour. When it does, ask yourself, "Do I like what I'm doing right now?" Or, "Do I dislike it but it's what is required to support the unfolding of my life?" (Examples might be doing your company books or changing your child's diaper.) Or, "Am I ambivalent, unsure?" Try to make brief notes on how you feel.

WHAT HAVE I ENJOYED MOST IN THE LAST FEW DAYS?

A game of tag, a moonlit stroll, praise from a co-worker, the first moments in a hot, fragrant bath? List as many as you can think of.

IN THE WEEK OR SO AHEAD, WHERE DOES MY LIFE FEEL TOO PINCHED, CRAMMED FULL, OR RUSHED?

You may answer, "Everywhere." Break it down to one area, one day, one specific upcoming or ongoing circumstance.

AM I WILLING TO DO ANYTHING TO ALLOW MORE ROOM FOR BREATHING AND FEELING IN THE DAYS AHEAD? AM I WILLING TO MAKE ANY OTHER CHOICES?

CQ challenges the voice that says, "I can't change anything." That is never true.

Insights

The first auntie is Ms. Insight. Her Jackie-O–style glasses are as penetrating as the Hubble Space telescope. Her favorite hobby is spelunking.

Feet propped up in my writing room one morning (avoiding writing), I reread an old journal. As I read, I was stunned at the plethora of insights I had written down, insights into a number of the puzzles of my personality and life. I was equally stunned to realize that, although I had recorded these insights months or even years before, I had done little to turn them into sustained action, to put flesh on them, to direct my life by their light. I had seen what I needed to do, but I hadn't done it. I swung my feet off my desk. Why was I wasting these sparks from God's mind? What would it take for me to heed their call?

Auntie Insight functions like a flashing neon beacon beeping. "Here is your unfolding path. Pay attention." Insights are the Divine nudging us into the flow of life. We all glimpse Ms. Insight all the time, but we don't consciously notice her or we conveniently forget her because, of course, she invites change into our lives and who *really* wants that?

Here's my list of insights, culled from journals, therapy, women's group, and the process of mindful questioning:

- I need to slow down and check in; the feeling of hurry is self-imposed; it's okay to let others wait or to take a time-out.
- When I feel myself getting controlling, I need to do something wild. Put on music, dance, go outside and look at the flowers, even if it is work time.
- Spiritual practice does not mean thinking about meditating or reading about praying. It means risking, slowing down, and opening to God. It means being

willing to sit with the messy and ugly parts of myself.

🪶 The dark spot inside needs body work, yoga, painting, poetry.

🪶 Lilly needs me to be still with her. She needs us to play, walk in nature, garden, at her own pace.

🪶 Each day needs creativity for the sake of love, not money, even if I just arrange flowers, decorate an envelope for a letter to a friend, leave a funny message on someone's answering machine.

🪶 I can exercise anytime, I don't have to wait for big swathes of time; a little counts, too.

🪶 It doesn't matter that I've been wrong or lazy about my health. I deserve to continue to explore health solutions; I won't give in to despair.

🪶 I can choose real self-nurturing instead of nervous half-present self-nurturing. I really do have a choice.

Screenwriter Randi Ragan had a powerful insight during a yoga retreat. She realized she wanted to stop eating meat, not for the reasons she had had before ("I had never practiced being a vegetarian from my heart, always from my intellect—it is better for the planet, et cetera," Randi explained) but because this time she grasped the principle of nonviolence. "There is a yoga principle called *ahimsa,* nonviolence on every level. There was a guy on the retreat and during this wonderful vegan meal we were eating, he said, "There is such loving energy in this food." Something shifted for me. It completely blew my mind, on this very deep level. I realized I must take care with the food I put into my body, that I don't want the violence in the food to come into my body. As I put my attention toward this insight, it has spread throughout my life, to my thoughts, to my speech, to my attitude toward insane drivers."

When you read about Randi's insight, your world is not rocked. You may think it sounds flaky, insignificant, or old news. You are not reading about someone who had a vision about working among the poor, then sold everything and moved to Calcutta. You can dismiss your own insights for this same reason: they don't sound like much. But this is what distinguishes them; this is why you must listen to them; when you think of your insight, for the first time or the hundred fiftieth, you taste inspiration. You feel a rustling of energy in your belly, a quickening, a spell being woven. You are a child, who very early in the morning, before she is fully awake, flickers with an enchanting, anticipatory, intoxicating feeling, the feeling that something good has happened. Then she remembers what it is and gets up to play with her new doll or to sneak out to see her favorite aunt sleeping with curlers in her hair on the couch. That's the same kind of feeling you look for in an insight. There is an exhilaration, a trueness, a feeling in your body of a bull's-eye.

Take a moment and slip on Auntie Insight's telescopic glasses and locate your insights. Your list need not be vast. Mine is a bit too long. Realistically, you can work with only one to three insights at a time, and you may work with these for years. Sometimes an insight is so mind-shifting or central to your life, or your energy is so low, or your children so young, that it is appropriate to choose only one insight and let it spread throughout your life, building on itself.

If you aren't sure about an insight, experiment. See what your body has to say. A little time and checking in with yourself will quickly tell you if you are working with a valuable, authentic insight or with something you think you "should" do.

If you take on too much, become goal-oriented and pushy about it, you will find tension headaches, a locked jaw, and little soul fulfillment. Instead, take it easy and focus on what feels right in your body, and you will find grace, miracles, and a soul growing into ripe beauty.

Here are some ways to locate Ms. Insight in your life:

Reread your responses to the questions so far. Track what you've been yearning for more of. Don't hesitate to start with simple, straightforward insights. Big words or loftiness does not an insight make.

Scan old journals. Don't read carefully. Instead, keep your eyes half focused and turn pages at a regular pace. Put half of your focus on what you are reading and half on what your body is saying about what you are reading. When you get a reaction, stop and make a brief note about what you read. Do this scanning for no more than fifteen minutes. When you are finished, write down the themes or words that emerged. Turn these over in your mind, see if they lend themselves to being formulated as an insight.

If you are in or have ever been in therapy, ask your counselor what insights she has heard you discover. Sit with these, retreat with them, see which ones spark your imagination. Some might be too vast or scary for you to tackle right now. There is spacious mercy in acknowledging this. Once, when I was sitting in the sun by Cold Springs Creek, a snake appeared and climbed up on a rock. It wasn't going anywhere. Neither was I—I wanted to stay by the creek, too. It felt good to keep one eye on the snake. Feels good to do that with insights I'm not ready for yet. Checking back in every now and then, keeping one eye open but not doing anything. Yet.

Ask several close friends what they have heard you express about yourself or what they've perceived is brewing in you. You might ask, "What have you heard me say I've realized about myself or that I want to work on?" Incorporate their ideas *only if it feels right in your body when you are hearing it. Don't borrow others' opinions until you thoroughly check them out yourself.*

Go on a retreat with the intention of asking, "What insights may I want to integrate into my life?" Incorporate movement and meditation into your retreat. Don't worry about any answers coming. Focus on the question—use it as your mantra. If anything really wants to break through, it will.

If you write down your dreams, go back and see what insights, old and forgotten or freshly mined, you can capture. Or ask for a dream to help you.

Recall rousing nonfiction books you've read lately (or meant to read) or any seminars you've attended (or meant to attend). Were there any principles, ideas, or tools in those books or seminars that you found compelling? Even a small, practical idea can be valuable, like "Eat more soy" or "Take five deep breaths every morning."

Ask yourself, "What qualities do my friends have that I wish I had?" Or "What qualities do I admire most in the people I respect?" See what your partner, friends, and family do that you love or hate. Therein lie clues.

Become a hollow listening woman. In privacy and silence—perhaps behind a locked bathroom door, in a warm tub with your ears underwater and your eyes closed—imagine that your body is a hollow vessel, a magnificent carafe waiting to be filled. Breathe and keep bringing your mind back to this image and feeling of spacious openness. Waiting to be filled. After a few minutes of enjoying this, ask—not tell but ask—your inner wisdom, "What insights want to fill my vessel?"

Do not—I repeat, do not—gather too many ideas. Stop when you have three to five insights. Avoid insights that feel boring or dutiful. Choose insights that challenge you, make your pulse beat like a jungle drum. Risk is appropriate. Lack of interest is not.

Whisper to yourself, "There is no right way. There is no one way."

Record the insights that make you sing, quake, or become silent. Write them down only if they feel juicy, clear, and *yours*.

Get some blank 3 ¥ 5 index cards. This is a variation of a Barbara Sher idea from her helpful book *Live the Life You Love*. You are going to write an insight on a card but before you do, consider each insight individually and ask yourself:

- Will integrating this insight help me lessen stress or discomfort in my life? If not, is that okay? (Sometimes more stress or discomfort is absolutely necessary to integrate an insight. As long as you acknowledge what you are venturing into.)
- Do I want to integrate this insight or am I doing it for someone else? If so, who? Is that okay? (I have insights about being a better mother for Lilly. That's different from having an insight to please someone or to fulfill someone else's idea of me.)
- Does integrating this insight make me feel that I am connected to and serving the Divine? (You may not know the answer to this one. Still, it never hurts to ask.)

🪶 Am I secretly hoping my life will change or be fixed by working with these insights?

🪶 Do these insights fit with my values and beliefs? Are they fair to others?

🪶 What reactions might the people closest to me have when I start practicing/living/embodying these insights?

🪶 Which insights do I feel most passionate about? Which ones, if they were in place, would help the other insights grow in me?

After you've done your sorting, take the insights that have passed the test (try to limit yourself to three to five) and rewrite them on the index cards as inspiring, direct "how can I" questions. Here is my revised list:

🪶 How can I slow down and check in, be more aware of my unfolding path?

🪶 How can I embrace the search for a spiritual practice?

🪶 How can I experience my creativity each day, for love's sake?

🪶 How can I continue to explore health solutions and not give in to my despair?

Clip your cards together—if you feel creative, you can decorate them—and carry them with you. Whenever you have time—waiting for an elevator, your child's karate lesson to end, the doctor to appear, your lunch date to show—read over your insights. Or keep them in front of you, post them by your desk, on your bathroom mirror, or inside your desk drawer. Read them often. When you forget or stop really seeing them, fine. Start again, move them someplace else, or rewrite them. Your insights will shift from time to time, will need rewording, refocusing. You will incorporate one and then you can drop it (although it might return later in a slightly different form). You might find you outgrow some, or that one or two aren't really you. Good! That's part of seeing the unfolding path and helping it to take its shape.

Contemplate your insights as you would koans or parables. Give your insights expression: make a ritual or a dance around one, or write a song or a poem. Offer them to the Divine in physical form. Embrace crooked thinking and the spiral nature of life. There is no room for "Have I got to do all this?" or "How will I master this?" Feelings do not keep pace with life's demands. They work on their own timetable. You are not initiating another list of demands on yourself for overnight change. You are simply becoming aware, paying attention, questioning. That's all and, truthfully, that's enough.

WHAT DO I LIKE AND DISLIKE ABOUT MY AFTERNOONS?

Again, use your prompt to remind you to tune in every hour or so during one afternoon. Ask yourself, Do I like doing this? Do I dislike it? Am I ambivalent?

WHAT IS ONE INSIGHT I HAVE DECIDED TO INTEGRATE INTO MY LIFE?

WHAT WOULD IT LOOK LIKE IF I SAW MYSELF CLEARLY INTEGRATING THIS INSIGHT?

Imagine what each of your senses, including visual, would apprehend. Imagine a few salient details that appeal to you.

HOW DOES THIS INSIGHT RELATE—OR NOT RELATE— TO WHAT I NEED MORE OF IN MY LIFE?

Go back to pages 12–13 and 63 to see if there is any relationship between what you wrote or thought there and your insights.

Ask

Insights Stir the Swamp

It is a glowing testament to my own denial that I have yet to face shadow comfort, the time monsters, or any of the other mangy, rank, disordered, gruesome, uptight, petty, sloppy, half-asleep in frog pajamas, marvelous, *essential* vampires that make creating our lives so entertaining and strenuous.

By choosing an insight and attempting to live it, and by simply putting more awareness in your life through reading this book, you stir your personal demon swamp. When you choose consciousness, when you choose to peer into the depths, you evoke parts of yourself that are damp, dusty, and dubious so that you can become more nearly whole. Shadow comforts and time monsters are the parts of you most in need of healing love and attention.

CQ pulls up a rocking chair beside my desk. "You're going to need my help for this," she says. "I've let you slide for too long. It's time to do your own peering. Why do *you* use shadow comfort so much? A bag of Rice Krispies bars will last you a day and a half. Why do you think that is?" I squirm under her gaze. "Then there is your obsessive spell checking and counting the spaces between a period and the start of the next sentence, a definite time monster. Or what about when your writing is going really well or you are so connected with Lillian and then you find yourself absolutely having to make a phone call. Why do you do that?"

"As I said before, shadow comforts, things like Rice Krispies bars and videos on Friday night are familiar, satisfying." I meet her eye defiantly. "They make me feel better."

A bag of Rice Krispies bars appears on my desk. "Here's a quote from your journal that contradicts you," CQ reads. "'Why do I eat? Because I'm afraid to

110

enjoy life. I eat to cut off what would be more satisfying but harder: intimate connection with Chris, being in my body, actually, any pleasure I truly, deeply enjoy. I almost feel as if I have to shut down, slow down, damper. . . . I am unable to fully grab life. *No,* no, not unable, afraid. What would happen? How would I be? I don't know what it looks like or what it feels like.'"

CQ produces a rose-colored cashmere shawl, wraps me in it, and hugs me. She croons, "The moment in which you choose to pick up the Rice Krispies bar is the creative moment. This is where you learn to two-step with anxiety. Everybody feels like Eva Peron on one too many espressos in this moment. You are not alone. But you've got to withstand that moment to create your life. The Rice Krispies bars, the shadow comfort, block it. This is where the gogo juice comes in, where the life unfolds, the Divine speaks, where you get hooked up to the universal power plant. When you block that, you block a lot. Instead of using comfort to block it, you've got to use comfort to become more comfortable in your own skin."

"Can I have one Rice Krispies bar?" I murmur through the cashmere.

"Come, sit in my chair." CQ gets up. I scoot over. "Close your eyes and rock," she tells me. "What you withstand by choosing to remain conscious makes you so much stronger. Invite the uneasiness in. Celebrate it, wrap it in ribbons, even if you also want to pull your hair out and slit your wrists. Make peace with it. Resist filling that space with shadow comfort. Refuse to make yourself smaller. Take this moment and experience it from a place of Mystery. The more you can invite Mystery, the more you are creating your life."

I gulp and breathe into the pit in my stomach. I try to concentrate on my breath instead of the Rice Krispies bars. I remember a therapist I saw when I was in my mid-twenties. She was always saying, "I need to sit with that," whenever I asked her a hard question. I thought that was such a curious statement. Is this what she meant? Wrapped in a shawl, rocking, trying to let go. Trying to withstand the desire to check out versus the desire to dive deep.

Deep into the moment. What was there? What feelings, ideas, choices . . . Fear. "I'm so afraid."

"That's why I'm here. We're all afraid. We run from this rich, ripe moment because it contains such aliveness. It makes you feel." She grasps my arm, then tickles it lightly. "It makes us aware how vulnerable and mortal we are. We want to deaden that awareness but in deadening, we deaden the ability to create our lives, to make conscious choices. Really, Jennifer, the most fundamental question we are faced with is how alive are we willing to be in the face of our own imperfections and failings, our fear of death, the world's suffering, innocent children's suffering, the whole motley, shitty, bewitching lot."

I start to cry—chest-heaving, nose-running sobs. CQ stays right beside me.

I get the feeling she isn't going anywhere.

WHAT DO I LIKE AND DISLIKE ABOUT MY EVENINGS?

How do you spend your evenings? How do you end your day? What makes you feel satisfied, at peace, pleased? Check in with yourself.

WHAT ARE MY FAVORITE SHADOW COMFORTS?

Make a list. No one need ever see it. If necessary, play detective for a few days and watch yourself. CQ reminds you, "Be courteous toward yourself. Shadow comforts will only shift from a place of self-kindness. Harshness will make things much worse."

WHAT ARE FOUR OR FIVE SITUATIONS OR FEELINGS THAT TRIGGER A SHADOW COMFORT RESPONSE IN ME?

Think of hurts, stress, and when you are being pushed to be more alive. For me, when someone rejects something I wrote, when I'm stuck in my writing, when I need to connect with Lilly or Chris but don't want to make the effort, when I'm trying to do something and keep getting interrupted, these are my siren calls to sweets or other distractions.

WHAT ARE MY MOST BELOVED TIME MONSTERS?

Some time monsters are things you create; some are things you need to become aware of so you can dodge them, at least occasionally. Perfectionist cleaning is a time monster you create. A gossipy co-worker is something you have to dodge.

Verve Talk

Mindful Mindlessness

Enough creating your life. Take a break from
RELENTLESS SELF-EXAMINATION.

Choose some healthy downtime. How can I write this after discovering that the very moment of creation, the big bang of our lives, the moment in which we choose to feel and listen, is missed if we check out?

Because I also discovered that awareness needs to be balanced (there's that pesky word again, can't seem to get rid of it) with unconscious consciousness, wildness, fecund fruitfulness, letting your mind wander where it may. Writer and environmentalist Thomas Berry believes there is a human need for extravagance. We can't be too straitlaced, tight-lipped, and frugal.

As we give up the duality of our lives (this is work and this is play, this is healthy food and this is food I really enjoy), as we move more to a middle position where everything is chosen out of self-love, then it doesn't feel like relentless self-examination. It feels like play.

Until then, we still need recess.

Embrace and give voice to all your needs and selves. In doing so, you can grow in self-trust. Because there are parts of you who hate the Comfort Queen. There are parts of you, like me, who use shadow comfort as proof you cannot be trusted. My inner critic badgers me with, "See what happens when you take some time off? See what happens when you nurture yourself? You eat the entire bag of Oreos or you lie on the couch all night watching TV. You can't be trusted." But when you *choose* a little wildness, a little healthy checking out ("choose" being the operative and all-important word, "healthy" being important, too), you show yourself that the sky does not fall when you stop to lie in the clover.

PERMISSION TO

Imagine CQ holding a big banner across the sky proclaiming, "Permission to bury this book under a pile of dirty laundry and go ride in a convertible, teeth gleaming, hair streaming." Or at least go to a matinee.

Forget creating your life for a few hours, days, or weeks. I'll still be here when you get back.

WHAT WOULD HAPPEN IF I OPENED MY HEART AND MIND TO
THE POSSIBILITY THAT MAGIC AND MEANING MIGHT BE FOUND
IN THE INTERRUPTIONS OF MY LIFE?

You've got to let your imagination run a bit on this one—and notice I say "might."
Think of the most annoying interruptions and then spend a moment searching for
their hidden gifts.

WHAT ONE THING COULD I DO WITH ONE OR TWO PEOPLE
IN MY LIFE TO SHARE COMFORT AND NURTURING?

Sheila said, "When I decided that self-nurturing wasn't going to be a treat but a way
of life, I had to shift from doing it alone to making it part of my relationships. I found
that my daughter and I could paint side by side, that my partner and I could bike
together, and that my mother and I could put together photo albums."

HOW CAN I PROVIDE FOR MY BELOVED SELF?

BASIC NEED: A meal of raw organic foods, a mammogram, new glasses, new under-
wear that doesn't creep, learning one thing about investing for retirement, saving
five dollars a week for a year . . .

PETITE TREAT: Trying out a new recipe, picnic on a weekday, chick flick on weeknight,
not answering the phone, new essential oil,
sending yourself a card . . .

TRAVEL: To a country fruit stand, the wind-
swept top of a tall building, a limestone cave, a
crumbling cemetery, an antiquated chapel . . .

How Do I Feel?

My friend Deborah is feeling resentful because her husband takes time for himself to play tennis and she rarely takes time for herself. "I don't know what questions to ask," she says. "I don't know what I want. I don't know what to ask for because it doesn't feel like anything is more important than what I'm doing, which is taking care of my daughter. I'm *supposed* to be doing this."

What do you want? How do you spend your time now, and how do you feel about your choices? These are the most basic questions we can ask ourselves. This is where creating our lives gets down to brass tacks. It is a frightening question because so often the answer can be "I don't like this aspect of my life" or "I don't feel much," and we have no idea what to do about it. Or the answer is "I love this so much" and we are afraid to feel that good! (We are such funny creatures.)

"Yes, honey, that's it! You've got to be willing to *look.*" CQ swoops into my study, carrying a breathtaking bouquet of delphiniums and bachelor's buttons. "First you concentrate on believing you are worth it while at the same time you are working on getting a touch of inner order in your life." CQ arranges the flowers in a tall vase, making a huge mess. "You've been doing a fine job on that front. Now it is time to say, 'What do I like? What don't I like?'"

"I like those flowers on the windowsill. I don't like the petals on the floor." I lean back in my chair. "I don't know. . . . Asking what you like and don't like, it all feels so self-indulgent. Navel-gazing, my grandmother would call it. You don't get to like everything about life. I certainly don't like being a parent when Lilly is in her terrible, whiny mood. I don't like being married when Chris and I are hiding from each other. There are parts of being a writer I detest."

CQ purrs, actually purrs, and smiles a smile Cleopatra would have envied for its subtle knowing. "Don't worry, my little Puritan, this is much harder than anything you've done before. It requires more than sentimental wishing; it requires real knowing, and blending in those atom-splitting heart-igniting questions, 'Why am I here?' and 'Whom do I serve?' But first come the observations."

I notice she is setting up a massage table. "How about a massage? Or are massages something you like?"

Her question stops me cold. Are massages something I like? They are something I am supposed to like, something I often wish I had more money for. Do I actually like them, and if so, what is it about a massage I like?

Intrigued, I climb onto CQ's table.

WHAT ONE THING COULD I DO IN THE DAYS AHEAD TO BECOME THE PERSON I MOST WANT TO BE?

One thing you *want* to do. Sometimes it takes a day or two of asking before you find what it is. That's okay. Sometimes you do one thing and realize that wasn't it. That's okay, too.

WHAT DO I FEEL I MUST DO IN THE DAYS AHEAD? WHAT IS WEIGHING ON ME, POKING ME, OR EATING UP MY TIME?

WHAT COULD I DO ABOUT IT?

Brainstorm for one minute about all the savage, politically incorrect, impetuous, weird things you *could* do.

WHAT AM I *WILLING* TO DO? WHAT AM I WILLING TO TRY?

Often I falter because I'm thinking about what I should do, but I have no intention of actually doing it. Or I stop myself from stretching as far as I could because I never stop to think, "What am I willing to try?"

write a dream image that inspires or intrigues you

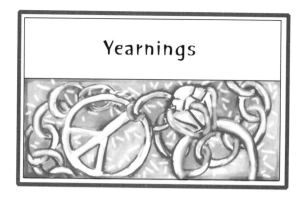

Yearnings

The second sister in the Auntie triumvirate is Ms. Yearning. Yearning has bottomless aqua eyes that beckon you to sit beside her and name your itches, daydreams, cravings, the flutters around your heart, the restless ideas that won't go away. Sometimes Yearning seems to be more scent than substance, an ever-changing and sometimes maddening concoction of dawn zephyrs, a newborn's milky breath, and sweaty sex. Her role is to help us find what we desire but may be afraid or unaware of wanting, or unable to want. The snippets of a song you sing over and over for days, the scent of a certain place, the memory of how a paintbrush feels in your hand, the reminiscence of how a Greek summer feels on your bare skin are all Yearning's nudges. Identifying her intimate treasures can feel like a poetic aphrodisiac, carrying all sorts of appetites to the surface, where you can unravel, buff, handpick or discard them, like a maharani choosing from among her luminous jewels.

Here is a list of my yearnings during the time I was writing this book:

- ✡ Create co-housing with other families.
- ✡ Write a truthful, helpful, funny book that will help me and other women with our daily lives.
- ✡ Create a deeper relationship with Chris.
- ✡ Work on parenting skills daily.
- ✡ Visit a spa with Chris.
- ✡ Go to Africa with Lilly and Chris.
- ✡ Go on a family wilderness trip.
- ✡ Finish the next stage of renovations on the house.
- ✡ Spend more time in nature.

✴ Do more engaging, alive things on the weekends.
✴ Feel energetic, clear, and healthy.
✴ Feel more open and expansive.

Collect your own list of yearnings.

For help casting your net wide, look back at the responses you had to these questions:

✴ What is my body saying right now about my life?
✴ What do I like and dislike about my mornings, afternoons, and evenings?
✴ What one thing could I do with one or two people in my life to share pleasure together?
✴ If I could do or be or feel anything in the coming days, what would it be?
✴ What one thing could I do in the days ahead to become the person I most want to be?

Go back to pages 105–106 and read over the list of questions that helped you locate your insights, but this time, substitute "yearning" for "insight." See what this search yields.

You can also locate yearnings by noticing where you are unhappy, unsatisfied, or stuck. What lessons keep coming up over and over again? What is the common theme of dissatisfaction in your life? What are your most persistent complaints? Go back and look at your responses to these questions:

✴ What could this stress or discomfort be asking me to develop?
✴ What intuitive knowing is rustling around in the back of my heart, lurking on the edge of my knowing?
✴ What is nagging me, hanging on the edge of my consciousness?
✴ What are my most common obstacles to relaxation and self-nurturing right now?
✴ What am I doing for myself that I could be doing for someone I love?
✴ What one issue in my life am I feeling two contradictory impulses about?

What patterns emerge? Could one of these patterns represent a yearning? A yearning that you are willing to explore, not for duty's sake but because you are in enough pain or passion to birth fierce desire? Take Jill, for example. She was having difficulties with her relationships. Two long friendships abruptly ended, and she wasn't making close friends in the city she had been transferred to. She blamed others and chalked it up to changing times (friends having babies, distance, etc.). But when she worked on her yearnings, she saw that although she yearned for closer friendships, all of the disappointments in her life had been about her friendships. Jill said, "For two of my yearnings, I wrote 'I yearn to have close friends' and 'I yearn to work on what is blocking my friendships.' What I found, over several months of working with both of these yearnings, was that being transferred to a new city had brought up painful memories from adolescence when I didn't fit in and protected myself by being like Dorothy Parker—funny, cutting, and very judgmental. I was now doing this same sort of sniping at my friends, new and old, and that was a big part of why I was having trouble deepening and maintaining friendships. There were, of course, other factors, but looking for yearnings from the perspective of my discontent made all the difference."

Here are a few additional ways to spot Auntie Yearning's signposts:

- Look for art supplies bought, woodworking projects started, sketches for your garden sanctuary shoved to the back of a drawer, file folders full of information about graduate school, summer retreat programs, travel adventures—search out the half-finished-not-enough-time clues.
- Listen to what you complain you never have time for. That's usually a yearning. If it isn't, stop complaining. If it is, put it on your list and prepare to do something about it.
- Pay attention to your dreams when you are doing this kind of reclamation work. They will often give you very vivid and clear clues.
- Investigate, recall what you loved to do as a child, a teenager, an adult, before kids or high-pressure jobs. Horses, acting, chess, swimming, playing Monopoly, listening to the Beatles . . . pleasures that you need in your life, just for their sake.

Some women can name what they want effortlessly. They can compose lists upon lists of dreams—"camel trip across Aussie outback, Peace Corps in Tanzania, attend a runway fashion show in Paris, learn Polynesian dance in Rarotonga." For others, especially those of you who you have been abused or are battling depression, recording your passions can be more forbidding. So before we go any further, let's scatter to the winds the idea that you have to know exactly what you want or how you want to feel to create your life. You don't. I repeat: *You don't,* I don't, none of us do.

You can choose yearnings even as you keep asking. You can grope your way toward where you want to be even when you feel unworthy or blocked, or when you doubt the depth of your desire. "I never stopped to ask myself," Jackie admitted when we talked in her office one spring afternoon. *That* is the sin, the blockage, the stumbling block we want to avoid. "I had never stopped to ask myself what I really wanted to do. I was more comfortable being in an okay job and complaining than asking myself, 'What do I really want?' It isn't an easy question to ask, and in the meantime I have to work to pay the bills, but it feels so good to be asking the question at all." Asking. Trying. Pausing long enough to go beyond the monkey mind until you can hear the Divine. This step can't be skipped. In the case of getting to know Ms. Yearning, it means stopping long enough, over days, weeks, months, and years, to ask "What do I like? What do I dislike? What do I want to grow toward? What am I being steered toward?" To stop assuming we know the answer before we even ask the question. To keep believing we deserve to ask.

Ironically, there is so much emphasis these days on being a wild woman, living our dreams, doing what we love and the money will follow, that we poor souls who aren't sure, who live with a measure of ambiguity and uncertainty, sometimes can feel that everyone else has a Publishers Clearing House truck at their front door. We need to keep fumbling our way toward what we desire, sitting with the unknowing, *without becoming paralyzed.* We can't give in to "I don't know what I want to create in my life so I'll do nothing," nor can we drain our days with complaining.

Look back over your responses to the questions. You've been doing the hard work of observing your life, so you have tons of material to start with. Gather bits and pieces of desires, sparkling fragments, or full-blown fervor. Begin your list.

AS I TAKE ANOTHER TURN ON THE SPIRAL OF MY LIFE,
WHAT AM I COMPLETELY, UTTERLY READY, TO BE RID OF?

What is the first thing that comes into your mind? Read it aloud and put it on the curb of your psyche to be hauled away.

Instead of _____, I could choose to _____.
Instead of _____, I could choose to _____.

In the first blank, write down a current time monster or active shadow comfort. Then breathe and ask yourself, "Is this what I really want?" If the answer is "No" or "I'm not sure," ask yourself, "What would satisfy my soul more?" or "What is this shadow comfort trying to teach me?" Feel CQ near you, perhaps patting your arm and murmuring, "All will be well, honey, all will be well."

WHAT COULD I LET GO OF DOING, THINKING,
OR FEELING IN THE DAYS AHEAD?

CQ leans into your peripheral vision, winks, and says, "What are you afraid to stop doing? What could you give up, even for a week, that would actually give you time to work on your insights and yearnings? Hmmm . . ."

Winnowing Your Yearnings List

Whether your list is long and strapping or tentative and pale, the challenge comes in making choices, deciding which yearnings are worth conscious effort and sacrifice. How much do you really want this? What are you willing to do? Which ones can you allow to slip through the cracks of your life (perhaps grabbing a taste on the way)? Which ones can you make family passions out of, which ones can you intertwine with or base your work on, and which ones take on a life of their own, claiming you?

Note: *Ms. Yearning is not particularly interested in lists of material things. Goodies are great but if we focus only on what we want, we will only succeed in fueling that hollow, fidgety consumer urge of wanting more. Ms. Yearning wants to fuel our spiritual growth so we serve our life purpose instead of our whims. Our deepest desires lead us away from being a number in someone else's marketing plan and toward being who we are, a who that doesn't fit into any brand designation. Judicious picking and choosing from our jewels of yearning keep us from chasing after yearnings that don't serve our souls.*

One by one, put your yearnings to the test of these questions:

✴ Does this yearning make me feel alive, engaged, present, and that I am serving the Divine, the purpose, of my life?
✴ Am I secretly hoping my life will change or be fixed by inviting this yearning into my life?
✴ What am I willing to give up to make time and energy for this yearning?
✴ How might the people closest to me be affected if I follow/allow this yearning?

✦ Which three yearnings do I feel I can't live without? Which ones, if they were in place, would help the others grow?

After you've done this sorting, choose one to five yearnings that have passed the test and rewrite them on your index cards as "how can I" questions. Here is my transmuted list:

✦ How can I create a more intimate, satisfying relationship with Chris?
✦ How can I pay more daily attention to improving my parenting skills?
✦ How can we go on a family wilderness trip this summer?
✦ How can I create co-housing with other families?
✦ How can I write a truthful, helpful, funny book that will help me and other women with our daily lives?

I dropped "Do more engaging, alive things on the weekends" because I was engaged enough with my work and this fit under working on connecting with Chris, as did spending more time in nature (Chris and I connect beautifully in nature). I realized that "Feel energetic, clear, and healthy" and "Feel more open and expansive" were covered by two of my insight questions. I hated dropping "create co-housing," so I wrote it on a card, guiltily knowing I really wanted it but didn't have time to pursue it. Later it occurred to me that it was something Chris and I could work on together. It also irked me to not include the renovations on the house. But after what CQ had been hammering into me about making hard choices, I knew trying to work on the house, or even *to think* about it, while seeking these other aspirations that I had deemed more important, would only cause that feeling of being pulled between two horses that are galloping in opposite directions.

Careful choosing invites us out of whining "I want this" into "Do I really want this?" and "When am I able and willing to do something about it?" We aren't able to stay in the fuzzy wanting, the endless cycle of never enough. We declare our desires, and paradoxically, in doing so, we invite simplicity and contentment into our lives.

When you are choosing which yearnings to pursue, it helps to remember that many yearnings have time restrictions. Take for example my choices of a family wilderness trip and my book: after we had found and paid for the trip, and after this book was finished, I would have time for other things, like house renovations. Choosing to *focus sequentially* in this way cleared considerable real estate in my brain. I wouldn't allow myself to go there in my imagination right now even to just fantasize about carpet colors. I kept bringing my power of focus, my intention, back to what I was creating (more about how to do this in the next section).

Structuring the yearnings as questions is the next step. This brings energy to the process and leads to deeper listening and taking action. In the past, when I wrote, "Go on a family wilderness trip," I thought, "Sure, that's a good idea." But I didn't feel inspired to do anything. "How can I go on a family wilderness trip?" engages my imagination, rubs up against me and asks, "What can you come up with?" It's a friendly challenge. It invites vision.

I keep my yearnings on little cards and posted as a list on my bulletin board. One day, talking on the phone, I glanced up at my list. At the bottom, I had written, "May I write a truthful, well-crafted, funny, helpful book." *May* I? Without knowing it, I had structured one of my yearnings as an appeal. I was asking for help. I married yearning to the ancient entreaty "God willing and the creek don't rise." In other words, if it's okay with the Divine, this is what I'll work toward. Thy will be done. A few weeks later, I read in *Seat of the Soul* by Gary Zukav "Consider your intentions and your meditations ... within the context of prayer. Be able to say within your intentions and your meditations, 'And I ask for guidance or help' and expect to get it. Expect to get it. Aside from your level of responsible choice of energy and how you form that into matter, the dependency on prayer assists you in pulling to yourself and invoking grace. . . . You must ask."

Write the yearnings you desire most deeply on your index cards as both "how" questions and as "may" questions. One of my cards looks like this:

✴ How can I pay more daily attention to improving my parenting skills?
✴ May I pay more daily attention to improving my parenting skills?

It's an interesting shift.

Remember, there is no right way to do this. Feel free to add in other systems of thought or your own ideas. This is a work in progress!

You may find that insights and yearnings overlap. That's good. In this overlap is the place where the Divine Intelligence is served, where the questions "What is whole-making?" and "Whom do I serve?" percolate and serve up not answers but guidance. That's part of crooked thinking. You need intention behind yearnings and insights supporting yearnings, and yearning in your intentions (Ms. Intention is on her way; you will meet the third auntie. They all work together.) As you build your index cards (with the passing of time and with experimentation) you see a vibrant, *flexible,* accurate sketch of what you want and where you are supposed to be emerging. It stops being about "When I get this" or "When I get there, everything will be okay," and it starts *becoming* "I am here now. I enjoy this, I need to do this, I wish to do this someday *and* I am here now, paying attention to and feeling gratitude for who I am and where I am *now.* I am listening. I am open to interruptions and changes in course. I am trying to be true to the larger energies and my values. I have an eye on the big picture and an eye on the now."

A creative framework of perceptive guidance. That's what you're building.

WHAT ONE YEARNING DO I CHOOSE TO OPEN TO IN THE DAYS AHEAD?

Choose just one.

WHAT WOULD IT LOOK LIKE IF I SAW MYSELF LIVING AND ENJOYING THIS
YEARNING, GIVING IT ROOM TO GROW AND TAKE ON A LIFE OF ITS OWN?
WHAT FEARS AND EXCITEMENTS COME TO MIND?

CQ says, "Remember, Ms. Anxiety and Colonel Fear have the gogo juice. Don't shut
them out and don't let them run the show. Almost everybody's wary of Auntie Yearning, but when you get to know her, she is the life of the party."

HOW COULD I NURTURE MYSELF IN WAYS
THAT WOULD CULTIVATE TRUST AND LETTING GO?

CELEBRATING THE SABBATH: It doesn't have to be Sunday or a whole day, but you
do need to devote more than an hour to your inner life and to the Divine.

SELF-AFFIRMING RITUAL: "Ritual gives us a sense of participation in the larger
order, the antithesis of which is the feeling of alienation. . . . The only way the gods
know we're asking for help is through ritual," observes astrologer and provocateur
Caroline Casey in *Making the Gods Work for You.*

PRACTICING CROOKED THINKING AND
LEARNING FROM INTERRUPTIONS:
Look for moments where you want
to push ahead, get things done, but
instead could decide to just let go.

A Few More Thoughts About What You Desire

Here is a passage from the Upanishads, the mystical scriptures regarded as the well-spring of Hinduism, with which Carol Flinders closes her book *At the Root of This Longing.*

> Here people do what they are told, becoming dependent on their country, or their piece of land, or the desires of another, so their desires are not fulfilled and their works come to nothing, both in this world and in the next. Those who depart from this world without knowing who they are or what they truly desire have no freedom here or hereafter. But those who leave here knowing who they are and what they truly desire have freedom everywhere, both in this world and the next.

When we ask, "What do I want?" or "What do I yearn for?" ultimately we must ask in the service of freedom. When I asked Priscilla what she had learned about creating her life and the role her long illness played in it, she told me, "The point of us being here is to be free. Whatever increases your feeling of real, genuine freedom is the right direction to go. The essence of it is that you are not conforming to someone else's expectations. You are not conforming to someone else's vision. You are free to pursue your own uniqueness." To live with our yearnings held against our chests, feeling their hearts beat in unison with ours, we have to be willing to risk knowing the truth.

A dear friend called me yesterday from Florida to tell me she has fallen in love with another man and was leaving her husband of twenty years. Their one child had just graduated from high school. She was giving up their extremely comfortable life and starting all over.

For hours after I got off the phone, my heart beat fast. I was afraid and thrilled for her, heavyhearted for her husband, and I felt as if someone had just opened Pandora's box. A tremor ran through me. She had picked up and left. She was risking it all. Why did that thrill me so, tickle my imagination? Did I want to do the same? No. What I wanted was that feeling of intimate, risky connection, of committed passion again, in my marriage and in my life. As I tossed and turned that night, I knew there was a huge wake-up call in my friend's action: follow my lack of freedom, follow my discontent.

Another side to Ms. Yearning.

Please don't think that by advocating freedom I'm saying, "Do exactly what you want and damn everyone else." We've already gone over that territory. Listening, discernment, checking out your actions with various sources, keeps you from becoming a sixties-style sybarite in a polyester cat suit. Let's shag, baby. And we have to be willing, when examining yearnings, to look at what we are afraid to give up.

In *The Invitation,* Oriah Mountain Dreamer tells a story of a ceremony she led on a women's retreat. The ceremony is an opportunity for each woman to surrender seven things she holds "as precious to her life, seven ways of seeing herself or being seen by others." One woman was very concerned that if she surrendered her attachment to wealth and to being a good wife, she would want to leave her husband. She wanted a guarantee that this wouldn't happen. Oriah answered, "There is no such guarantee. If there were, there would be no point to doing the ceremony. I cannot tell you in advance what your choice will be, whether you will look at your husband and your marriage and know that it is a place you truly want to be. Your attachment to money and being the good wife may be all that's keeping you there." The other women did *not* like this response. One asked, "Why would we risk the unknown changes that this knowledge could bring into our lives?" Oriah considered before answering, "For freedom. I risk it for the freedom, to see what is true, what I really want in the deepest part of myself. I can make whatever choices I want in my life, and I will live with the consequences of those choices. But if I want to live a life close to my deepest desires, I have to risk knowing who I really am and have always been. Knowing this, I can choose."

"Okay, okay, enough with this deep talk about desire and freedom," CQ says, coming out onto the deck, where I am writing longhand in the sun. She hands me a glass of iced tea and plunks herself down in the patio chair next to mine. Before she speaks, she closes her eyes, breathes deeply, sips the tea, and breaks into a smile. "There, that is a genuine pleasure, an organic like. Don't ever forget that God speaks to us in pleasure, as well as challenges and growth pains. Our genuine desires and yearnings, they don't feed the greed that is destroying our world *if* we keep listening. As women get friendly with their true yearnings, which are constantly changing, they see that their pleasure doesn't destroy but creates: energy, beauty, community, love. It couldn't be more different from mindless shopping. However, teasing out the authentic is constant, painstaking work."

"But what about what Oriah was saying, about giving up your most cherished desires to be sure they *are* your most cherished desires?"

CQ hands me a glass of tea. "It's all the same thing. You can't hide behind false or outgrown desires after you begin to truly encounter what you want and start to consciously choose. The outmoded, false ones clash with the genuine, and eventually, they lose." She looks pensive for a moment. "Granted, it can be a very ugly battle." She smiles at me. "Now, stop thinking and try the tea. Close your eyes. Taste."

I close my eyes and raise the glass to my lips. I feel the perspiring glass, then the blush of tea—brisk, tingly, astringent against my teeth. Goose bumps flood my tongue; then a burst of flavor caresses me. Mangoes? Black sand beaches? Tropical tea plantations? Exotic images run through my mind's eye too fast to do anything other than be enjoyed. I swallow, and a spurt of frost shoots down my throat.

"See," CQ whispers. "Pleasure can simply be pleasure, pure and unadulterated, not addictive and not a spiritual practice. Sometimes what you like is simply what you like. It's okay to craft a life with a lot of what you like in it. It might not always be possible, but don't feel guilty while you're in the moment of pleasure."

A breeze trembles the wind chimes that hang under the eaves. "Be there and sip your tea. Just be there," CQ adds.

WHAT ARE THE THREE OR FOUR THINGS I THINK ABOUT MOST?

When Anna asked us this question in our women's group, I was distressed to see that mine were Lilly being hurt or killed, me becoming rich and famous, and my body falling apart.

IS THIS WHAT I WANT TO THINK ABOUT?
DO I WANT TO CHOOSE OTHER THINGS TO FOCUS ON?
IF I DID, WOULD I BE TRYING TO BE A "GOOD GIRL"?

Your list may reveal hidden desires, fears, and outer-focused obsessions.

HOW IS MY BODY COMPLICATING OR HELPING
MY ABILITY TO CREATE MY LIFE?

Moods, energy levels, handicaps, cricks, body image . . .

WHAT'S GOING ON WITH ONE OR TWO OF MY INSIGHTS?

CQ chuckles, "Perhaps you haven't looked at those little cards since you wrote your insights down. That's okay, give them a gander right now. You might find that, without knowing it, you've been working on them anyway."

Intentions

"Intention will give you the juice you need to keep going," CQ intones. "I'm off to fly fighter planes in forbidden countries with men with abundant mustaches and broad shoulders. Cheers." CQ gives me the queenly wave: stiff arm, hand rotating from the wrist, as she burns rubber in a red convertible, a seriously younger man in the passenger seat.

I'm left home alone with Auntie Intention.

Insight invites you to peer deep into where you could stretch more. Yearning is expansive, daring, concerned with pleasure and hidden creative potential. Intention is the third of the Auntie goals, and she powers the whole clan. It is Intention who wakes the sisters in the morning, handing them a cup of organic English Breakfast tea and reminding them why they want to accomplish what they've set out to accomplish. Intention is gogo juice concentrate: Just add attention and you'll have enough to last you for a long time. Intention knows that she carries a name fraught with meaning—she has been associated with everything from good intentions to future intentions to final intentions. She stays grounded by remembering how she defines herself: "an aim that guides action."

Intention knows that no yearning is going to become a reality, no insight is going to blossom unless you bring what you desire into alignment with what you think and feel.

Say I'm walking my usual route, up steep Cold Springs Road, past the college, and onto curvy, funky Mountain Drive. As I walk, I listen to music, try to break a sweat, and fantasize about the future. About how great everything is going to be when I finally stick to my low-carbohydrate eating program, when I exercise four times a week, when Chris finds his dream work, when the house is finished, when we get to Africa. When we observe our thoughts, we find that much of what we think about is boring, repetitive, and pointless. The kind of thinking, or really nonthinking, that I experience on my walks doesn't help me create my life, doesn't create anything but discontent.

Acupuncturist Carolyn Atkinson describes it this way, "Intention brings hope into the present, intention is hope in the here and now." Gandhi said, "What you think, you become." Deepak Chopra wrote in *The Seven Spiritual Laws of Success,* "Intention . . . triggers transformation of energy and information. Intention organizes its own fulfillment." To create our lives we must focus our attention on what we wish to create. So what, you may snort. I've tried that. I did, too. In the past, I visualized what I wanted, repeated my affirmations, glued together my wish collages. It never worked very well. I always worried, "Am I visualizing the right thing in the right way?" and "Is this really, really what I want?" I would go to sleep at night repeating that New Age phrase, "May this or something better happen for the greatest good of all concerned" and then worry I wasn't getting that part right, either. It all made me quite jumpy and squinty eyed. As my friend Kris said, "I do believe we can program the subconscious. I can say 'I am thin' a hundred and fifty times a day and I will get thin. It takes effort to do it properly and technically. It takes a lot of focus and time, and I've certainly done it. But I don't want to do it that way anymore. It feels like I'm forcing my will, forcing my life's direction. Is this really in my best interest?"

Here's the crucial difference: Instead of focusing your mind on the *details* of what you want (the living room right out of *Architectural Digest,* the taut thighs, your paintings hanging in a Manhattan gallery), focus on *how you want to feel when those things are a reality.* That's what Auntie Intention is all about: the feelings behind your dreams.

What helped me understand this more clearly was reading Elia Wise's *Letter to Earth.* When I read her question "How will I feel living this dream?" I became very excited. Of course, I thought! I had been using my will to try to create my ideal life and that felt awful. What if I used my will to focus on how I wanted to feel and stopped micro-managing the details?

This is the way Auntie Intention wants you to practice intention. Take your list of insights and yearnings and quickly read over what you wrote. As you do, imagine how you will feel, emotionally and physically, when each insight or yearning has come to fruition. Jan reported that "I read over my insights and yearnings, I read about my desire for forgiveness, creative fulfillment, more patience with my children, and gradually this picture of how I want to feel emerged. At first, I kept focusing on how I wanted my life to look, what possessions I wanted to have, or how things would be different physically. But that felt too specific and controlling, so I kept bringing my attention back to how my body would feel when these things are true. I would picture scenes but loosely. I would try to let the details go and focus on the feelings. I came up with a great emotional symphony."

I read over my yearnings and insights of the moment:

- How can I create a more intimate, satisfying relationship with Chris?
- How can I pay more daily attention to improving my parenting skills?
- How can we go on a family wilderness trip this summer?
- How can I write a truthful, helpful, funny book that will help me and other women with our daily lives?
- How can I slow down and check in, be more aware of my unfolding path?
- How can I embrace the search for a spiritual practice?
- How can I experience my creativity each day, for love's sake?
- How can I continue to explore health solutions and not give in to despair?

After I got over feeling overwhelmed by my too long list and chose to focus on only three items, I realized the feelings my yearnings and intentions had in common were spaciousness, light, alive, engaged, doing the right thing at the right time, trusting myself, and forgiving. (At first, I wrote "no guilt," but I transformed that into trusting myself, which is easier to feel.) That is how I want to feel in my life.

You might quip, "And who the hell doesn't?"

I'm not proposing that you will always feel this way or that you use this tool to mask real anger, guilt, or frustration. That's Mr. Denial, an entirely different customer. And just because you focus your mind on certain feelings, that doesn't mean you create exactly that by noon tomorrow Eastern Standard Time. It may take a long time. It may never happen because it isn't what your soul has in mind for you. But the perfect thing about Ms. Intention's method is *it doesn't matter.* It's the process of focusing your emotional being that counts. It protects you from "be careful what you wish for because you just might get it" because you are constantly going inside and listening to how you want to feel and letting that be the guide.

And another benefit of listening to your Auntie is she provides another route to divine balance. When I listen and focus on how I want to feel, I am naturally drawn to what I need to do each day to create a life that fits those feelings.

It's another day, another walk up Cold Springs Road. When my mind pings off into the future, I corral it back to the spacious, light, trusting-myself place. I might get there by thinking about a specific yearning or an insight, musing about how to make this aspect more a part of my life, what actions to take, and then let that carry me inside the feelings. Some days this works wonders, and I find myself opening, trusting, flowing, *without* the exterior of my life changing. The exterior hasn't changed yet. I'm already there emotionally. And let me tell you, that feels very, very good. Other days, my obsessional nature wins and I'm lost in fantasies of smooth skin, a tidy garden, and my name on the *New York Times* best-seller list.

When you find yourself worrying, projecting into the future, obsessing about desires that aren't authentic (or written on your index cards), sitting with your demons, or simply trying to get the energy to take some action in your life, focus on how you want to feel. It is your personal magnifying glass focusing the awesome powers of your imagination and mind.

Auntie Intention is the aim that guides you *to* action.

WHAT WORDS DESCRIBE THE AIM THAT GUIDES MY ACTION?

Your intention is what I call "beyond words," and it isn't possible or even useful to define it. Yet it is helpful to choose a few words that can act as triggers to call up the feeling you are aiming toward. You could write these words on the backs of your index cards. My words: *trusting, leaping, looking all around, brow and shoulders relaxed, stopping, connecting.* Jan's: *laughing, baby's hands, in the flow of work, celebrating.*

WHERE MIGHT I APPLY CROOKED THINKING OR LOVE OF INTERRUPTIONS TO MY LIFE IN THE COMING DAYS?

Where might it actually be better to take the long route or to not know where you are going to end up? What gift could an interruption bring? My best friend, Barbra, calls to check in, in the middle of the day. At first, I'm antsy, wanting to get back to work. Then I give in to utter enjoyment. I discover when I hang up that I have a new idea and a fresh way into a piece I'm writing.

WHAT IS ONE THING I COULD DO TO SHARE JOY WITH TWO OR THREE OF THE MOST IMPORTANT PEOPLE IN MY LIFE?

What is your common ground? Where do your definitions of joy intersect? Not forcing or cajoling, but finding the intersection to share. Janice took Bach concertos to work to play for the two women she works with. Michele went horseback-riding on the beach with her niece and nephew, something they had all wanted to try. Stephanie took her kids for ice cream in the middle of the week. "Sweets are a big deal in our house," she said. "When I suggested we each have as much as we wanted, including banana splits, well, it was joyful."

Glass Half Full

The other morning, Joanie, a mom at our preschool, asked me offhandedly as we were latching the gate behind us, "What are you up to these days?" Without pausing to take a breath, I went into a well-rehearsed angst routine. "I'm giving a speech in front of three hundred people this week, I've got a big meeting next week, and I'm stuck rewriting the beginning of my book over and over again. I'm so worried that I won't get it right, and we haven't even looked at our taxes, and Chris has been gone for eight days, and Lilly was sick and then I got a touch of it...." Joanie backed off, probably afraid the foam forming at my mouth was laden with the insanity I was obviously infected by. I got into my car, feeling pontifical and brisk. Aren't I important! As I was driving home, I had the feeling something was not quite right. It took checking in with myself quite a few times over the course of that day before I got it. I had presented what I was doing as bad, stressful, too much. I shaped it into a drama. Yet that wasn't how I felt. Just under the surface, I felt aroused, purposeful, happy to have something to do after years of wandering around wringing my hands and bleating, "I'll never work again." Underneath the surface, I felt in alignment with my intention. But on the surface, it was *Bleak House, General Hospital,* Drama 101.

When we begin to inhabit our intention, we will encounter discrepancies between what we are working toward and how we are actually acting.

This is inescapable.

It's as if you've moved across town and then one day you find yourself pulling into your old driveway, having driven there from work without even knowing it. The old route is tattooed on your brain.

I was stuck in my familiar groove of feeling scattered, overwhelmed, unhappy. Sure, I was nervous about speaking in front of three hundred people. Sure, I'm always afraid that my writing won't be good enough or get finished on time. Here was ambivalence and complexity winking right at me. Still enslaved to perfection, I complained about what wasn't right, refused to stand up straight and say, "Today I'm doing lots of different things and I love that." I damaged my emerging strength and squandered the budding energy of my intention by sticking to the old stories, *even though I didn't believe them anymore.*

A few days later I'm sitting with Kristina at my dining room table. Our children rumble in and out of the room. Kris is talking about her move to Santa Barbara two years before and how difficult it has been. "What I've come to understand is that when I go into my soul and see the reason I wanted to move here, it was to raise children, to feel safe, to be around nature. I saw myself doing more art, quietly and on my own. But getting what I wanted has made the ego part of me very uncomfortable." She whines dramatically, "I don't have enough friends, I can't seem to find my tribe." Then she laughs. "In other words, I'm looking at the glass half empty. If I really look at it, I'm creating exactly what I imagined. I lost sight of this because I was so busy being uncomfortable. But it is happening in spite of myself, this more quiet life.... It is not ego-fulfilling all the time to be a great mother, but it is what I planned and wanted."

Kris's comments reminded me how important awareness is, both for keeping us on track and for nurturing our gratitude. I go into my office and get a copy of an e-mail I received from a reader, Kathy. I hand it to Kris who, being a very accomplished actress, reads it aloud to good effect: "'I think a woman who does not have the responsibility of children can, in fact, create a life for herself. I am writing this whilst yelling at three young boys, and I can tell you that I live vicariously through my alter ego who is a cross between Emma Peel of *The Avengers* and Frances Mayes who wrote *Under the Tuscan Sun,* with a little Martha Stewart thrown in for good measure! I imagine going to the market every morning and picking out the most glorious vegetables that appeal to me, without once thinking, Forget it, they won't eat that. I envision a house that smells of beeswax and lavender instead of urine and sneakers. I also see an impossibly cool woman in her forties who actually has the time to exercise and can wear Emma's black leather getup without having liposuction first. Reality, however, as they say, bites. I am neither hip nor cool, and my house stinks to boot! But I do dream of a day when my life will be a blank slate again, and I will decide who and what my soul is telling me to be. I also remember that twenty years ago, my heart was longing to be who I am today, and I guess that is a comforting thought.'"

Kris sips tea and says, "Maybe we think following the life we are creating means it will always feel good. But in reality, it may mean the part of us that was in charge, and loved being in charge, isn't anymore."

I smile at her, "That does not go over well with our inner control freak. She gets pissed off and tries to ruin the whole show."

Kris, Kathy, and I were all experiencing the *reality* of creating our lives. "It doesn't feel as comfortable as you imagine it will," Kris concedes. It all sounds so rousing and vigorous when we are planning, writing down yearnings and musing over insights, setting our intention. But yearning for a child and spending the next eighteen years raising her, it does try one's visionary abilities. The same goes for starting a business, a marriage, getting well, sticking with a spiritual practice, just about anything worth doing. Following your unfolding path, even getting your heart's desire, always involves wading through a whole lot of cow pies. To think otherwise is to live in New Age airy-fairy land. As many wise people have said, the soul is not concerned with your being comfortable; it is concerned with fulfilling its destiny. Which is why comforting yourself helps you find your soul!

To protect our emerging strength, it helps if we stop telling the same old stories. We all have our routines; like actors, we recite our lines over and over, and after a while, we stop listening to what we are saying. I knew something wasn't right when, during my pit tenure, I would regularly hear myself telling the story of why we couldn't have a second child because we both worked. It isn't that there wasn't truth in what I was saying—there was—it's that anything we repeat over and over is telling us, "Look at this. Stop talking, go inside and listen. Do not accept what you are saying as the truth. You are making a box and you will bury yourself in it if you aren't careful." When we tell the same old stories, we aren't saying, "It is what it is." We are buttressing our fears, instead of opening, listening, and accepting.

Rumi wrote of a man who prayed constantly until someone said to him, " 'So! I have heard you calling out, but have you ever gotten any response?' The man had no answer for that. He quit praying and fell into a confused sleep. He dreamed he saw Khidr, the guide of souls, in a thick green foliage. 'Why did you stop praising?' 'Because I've never heard anything back.' To which Khidr replies, 'This longing you express *is* the return message.' " When we forget, when we play it small, we rattle on about the same old shit. Instead, we can zip our lips and look for that sweet longing again. This longing tells us where the path is. The danger is when the longing becomes nothing but whining. Even so, Rumi cheekily reminds us to "Listen to the moan of the dog for its master. That whining is the connection."

WHAT IS NAGGING ME, HANGING ON THE EDGE
OF MY CONSCIOUSNESS?

What do you need to become aware of? It could be someone's birthday, a friend who needs loving attention, or perhaps you need the attention.

HOW DO I FEEL ABOUT
THE CHOICES I'VE BEEN MAKING LATELY?

Deciding it is possible to create your life is all well and good, but then it comes down to the nitty-gritty: what choices am I making from day to day? How am I spending my time? "Forget the big-ticket items for now," CQ pipes in. "It's easy to get your panties in a knot about the big chunks of time. Look instead at the junctions of your life, the hours between work and sleep, children and alone time. What are you choosing there? Where is that time going? Observing and choosing differently in these nooks can be mighty interesting."

HOW MIGHT I CONNECT THE CURRENT SEASON
WITH ONE OF MY YEARNINGS?

I yearned to go on a wilderness trip with my family. Walking early every morning for a week and observing not my monkey mind but the quality of the air on my face, the birds' behavior, what was in bloom—this helped fuel my fierce desire to fulfill this dream.

Verve Talk

More Comfort Queen Stories

Welcome yourself back into the circle of couches and rockers. The candlelight makes everyone appear tender and relaxed. Tea and champagne await you on a low table in the middle of the circle. Ambrosial chocolates are passed and shared like communion wafers. Silence descends. Breathing deepens.

Gillian tucks her legs underneath her and begins to tell her story: "I was staying in a small town far from home, healing from a trauma. I was feeling pretty lonely, thinking, What am I doing here? I didn't know anyone besides the therapist I was working with. I went downtown to get a coffee, to be near people. As I was walking down the street, I noticed an African-American woman coming toward me. The woman stopped, looked me right in the eyes. I'll never forget her look, it was so bare. She said, 'I'm afraid.' I asked her if I could help. She said, 'Can you pray with me? I'm a recovering alcoholic and I want a drink really bad. I'm from Sacramento, I've never been more than fifty miles from my home, and there are no black people here. I'm here to met my best friend and I can't find her. I'm really scared.' I took her hand and we prayed, and we walked down the main street of this little town, holding hands and praying. At the end of the street, the woman turned to me and said, 'I was praying for an angel, and you came. You're my angel.' I was high for the rest of the day because of her. She was so brave. She was as much an angel to me as I was to her."

Someone leans forward to pour another cup of tea. Outside, it begins to rain. After a moment of quiet sipping, Susan's voice emerges from the candlelight shadows: "A few years ago my husband and I moved to the suburbs because we had a three-year-old and were about to start trying to have a second child. We figured we would avoid paying for private school. We moved to New Jersey because I was working there. A year and a half later, I was not pregnant, and my company was moving to Minnesota. I chose not to follow. We were all happy in New Jersey, someplace I had *never* planned to live. I took a new job and was happy, except for a challenging relationship with my boss. During this time, I began working with two homeopaths to help me get pregnant, as well as traditional fertility doctors, whom my gynecologist said were probably my only hope. My second week at my new job I learned that my brother had two weeks to live. I began traveling to the hospital daily. The fertility appointments made me late to work, and visiting my brother made me leave as soon as was acceptable, so my time commitment to my new job did not impress anybody.

"Miraculously, my brother recovered," Susan continued. "He didn't even get the lung and heart transplants we were told he would need—a reminder that doctors don't know everything—and I quit the fertility doctors, committing myself to homeopathy, believing that if I made my body healthy I would be able to create a healthy baby. Traveling to New York and working in New Jersey was too stressful, and I didn't like 'forcing' my body to get pregnant; it didn't feel right. Within eight months, I had been fired. My ego bruised because senior management hadn't recognized a conflict between me and my boss and hadn't figured out a way to keep me, I decided to use the time to do some soul-searching.

"I starting seeing a psychologist. Together we learned I was following this 'idea' of what I had 'planned' to do and had stopped reevaluating my situation to determine if I still wanted the same things. I had always thought that career was most important to me, but now I had an amazing husband and a five-year-old daughter. I realized all I wanted to do was to be home focusing on raising my daughter without work being in the equation of balancing child-rearing and being a wife, homemaker, and friend. And I added something new to my life requirements, something I had pushed aside for a long time: my happiness. A big part of that happiness was to no longer punish myself for not being able to do things the right way. For example, I've always felt I should be able to lose weight without spending a lot of money, and since I could not figure out a way to do it, I stayed fat. Now I gave myself the permission to take tennis lessons and play weekly, as my husband had for years, and because that was an enjoyable form of exercise I lost twelve pounds! I gave myself permission to go to a workshop on getting in touch with my psychic self just because I wanted to.

"Suddenly I was a priority, and I found myself getting happier. Between the homeopathy, psychology, Oprah's suggested books, and my growing openness to the unknown (could there really be angels, and wasn't my wanting there to be some enough to allow me to enjoy the thought that there could be some?) I realized that I had taken to an extreme the control we do have in our lives. I had been blaming myself for all my imperfections, telling myself that I could not have any rewards until I had fixed them: I am overweight, and it is a waste to buy new clothes until I'm thin. But I didn't feel good about myself in my old clothes, which of course made it harder to lose the weight. Now I am telling myself I am worth the new clothes, because it will help me to get to next week. Now I am telling myself that I could not control everything, and to be open to the possibilities that come with unexpected outcomes.

"When I lost my job, it dawned on me that I was angry about not being home to raise my daughter. My husband and I accepted that we might not get pregnant again and made our peace with it. We went on vacation, took a class in reflexology which taught us what to do to stimulate my ovaries. We decided to get a dog to give me a 'baby' to nurture. Then my daughter told me that I would not get pregnant until we prayed to God. I had never given myself permission to pray to God to get pregnant because it seemed too self-serving. The new me prayed to God with my daughter.

"Within two weeks I was pregnant (we put off getting the dog). In my first trimester I was told at one point that numbers indicated that I had miscarried. I was very sad, but I prayed, saying I trusted that there must be a reason, and surprisingly I did not feel devastated. An hour or two later the doctor's office called back to say there had been a mistake and I was indeed pregnant. It was at that moment that I felt that 'I got it'—that I had to truly let go in order to receive. It was an amazing moment. I now have a second beautiful daughter. I plan on sharing my experiences with her in a way that will help her to appreciate that there is no one right way, as well as the wonders we experience every day, every hour, and every minute."

Every head in the room nods in agreement.

"This is a long one. You sure you want to hear it?" Several women get up and to go the bathroom or get water. After everyone settles down again, and silence comforts the room, Domenica begins: "I spent a good twenty years of my life working in social service programs. The last work I did was as a research analyst for a large corporation. About ten years ago, I had been working sixteen-hour days, and my body started breaking down in a very particular way. I started having dreams that I was dying. Not dying in a physical way; something within me was dying. I really listened to the voice inside me, and I made the choice to leave my life—a house I loved, a job that was highly prestigious, the best income I'd ever made. I did it because I knew if I didn't, whatever I was meant to do or become or grow into, was simply not going to show itself. I left my life, did a bunch of side trip things and ultimately ended up in Santa Fe. There I met someone who told me about a retreat. It was very expensive, I could not afford it, yet my entire body said, 'Do this no matter what.'

"I went on the retreat, and there I met a woman who led me to my guru, who brought me to the healing work I now do. I met a man who got me a job as a caretaker for a property up on a mountain. I was basically alone and therefore able to complete my shift into the renunciatory form of life I now live. The guidance for all this was, as I say, very, very contrary to what people would have you do in the world. When I left my job, for instance, the people I worked with were aghast, 'My God, what's going to happen to you? You're throwing your life up in the air! You're a single woman, you don't have any backing or family.' Natural, instinctive concerns.

"Ten years into my new life, I started getting the same feeling in Santa Fe. I had a full practice in Santa Fe, a very beautiful home that I loved, and a group spiritual practice that was extremely important to me. But there was another very strong message saying, 'Leave and go back out into the world. Take the work I am doing and go be an instrument in the world in a very different way. When I began to ask where I was supposed to go, I heard 'southern California.'

"I moved to Los Angeles and had a series of awful experiences. I just felt blocked and confused at every turn. I left there, and I've basically been homeless, staying on friends' couches and at the ashram, for almost a year. But every time I look in the paper for an apartment, my body goes berserk. It's basically telling me, 'That's not the way this is going to happen. If you proceed and try to make it happen in that way, wrong things will happen.' Those are the kinds of voices we need to listen to. The creation of my life right now is about sitting in the unripe place and not trying to push to make it ripe. It is the difference between creation and willfulness, the fine edge of watching myself all the time. I keep calling people, I keep making contacts, I tell people what kind of life I'm looking for, what kind of work I do, and I hope to help it occur when it is time."

The women hold Domenica in respectful silence, perhaps thinking of the many times in their lives when the path has remained unclear, the unripe place claimed them for almost longer than they could endure.

What story would you tell in this circle?

WHAT QUESTIONS ARE BEING STIRRED IN ME?

It may be time for you to come up with your own question. It might be "Why do I let myself get so crazy when my boss is around?" Or "What am I getting out of telling myself I'll never make it as artist?" Or _____. Listen for the question of this time.

HOW HAVE I BEEN TALKING TO MYSELF?
WHAT IS THE DOMINANT THEME IN MY HEAD?

Just because we decide to use intention doesn't mean we won't ever have a demeaning or derailing thought again. All we can do is keep checking in and gently reframing the way we speak to ourselves. CQ calls from the other room, "'Gentle' being the operative word. Don't use your Mr. Critic or Mr. Should to get your mind back on Auntie Intention."

HOW CAN I HOLD MYSELF IN MY HEART IN THE DAYS AHEAD?

ONE RESTORATIVE, UNABASHEDLY BALLSY, COWGIRL THOUGHT: "Every day I am able to listen to my heart, test out my perceptions in the world, and follow my unfolding life with courage"—that is one possibility.

COMPASSION FOR MYSELF: When my friend called about her anxiety attacks and kept saying, "I don't know what's wrong with me, I don't know why they won't stop," I said, "They won't if you keep beating yourself up for having them."

A FEW MOMENTS OF BREATHING INTO A FEAR OR GRIEF: Sitting and breathing, not running, not making bargains, not dramatizing it and making it the center of your life.

Faith

"I'm wondering when you are going to write about faith."

I'm taking a break on the tiny deck nestled in the fold of our roof, eyes closed, the sun nuzzling my face. We've had a long winter, and today is the first fine day in weeks. CQ leans over me and I open my eyes in the cool shadow she casts. She winks, then sits down in the plastic lawn chair we keep up here. I close my eyes, rubbing them with my fingers until my eyelids explode in a kaleidoscope of psychedelic designs.

"Faith? What in the world would I have to say about faith? Did you turn into Pat Robertson while I wasn't looking?" I crane my head around to be sure CQ is still CQ.

"What happens when your life isn't unfolding?" CQ replies, ignoring my dig. "What happens when you don't hear anything? What happens when you can't go it alone anymore, when you are faced with horror or disappointment so keen you are certain you can't go on? Then how will you create your life?"

I take my hands off my eyes and look at her. "I thought we had covered all this—everything isn't predetermined, it's what you make out of what life hands you."

"I did say that. Very neat, isn't it? What happens when you are alone in your bedroom at 3:00 A.M. with the news you've got breast cancer? What are you going to do when your father dies? Or if you found out Lilly had a brain tumor? What's going to help you make something redemptive out of that?" CQ expands a bit and takes on a fiery glow.

I sit up and stare at her, dumbfounded. "What's gotten into you?"

"The way I am talking to you is exactly the way you talk to yourself whenever you desire the Divine, when you want to melt into God. You stop yourself. You are able to write about the larger energies, the invisible forces, for pity's sake; you are even able to *see* me. But when it comes to falling into the arms of the Divine, when it comes to surrendering your reason, when it comes to having faith that you are not alone, you hold back. You get defensive and prickly."

My heart is beating fast. I realize that throughout this adventure with CQ, I've had the uneasy feeling that I'm dodging something. Skirting the issue. Hiding.

Leave it to CQ to expose me to the light.

"I don't see why we have to talk about this."

"Jennifer, my beloved, don't do this." CQ sits down and puts her arms around me.

For the first time, I move away from her. "I'm going to stretch a little, I'm so tight from sitting at the computer."

"Don't you realize that what you are feeling is what almost everyone feels? Even the ones who go to church, even the ones who lead the churches. Everyone is faced with this question over and over. Is the universe a benevolent place? Am I connected to something infinite, and does that infinite something care about being connected to me?"

I straighten up from stretching my calves and glare at her. "I am not qualified to write about this." I'm angry now. More than angry, I'm seething.

"Why not?'

"Because I—I don't know—because I'm not smart enough. I haven't gone to a seminary. I play at my spiritual practice, I don't wipe the noses of the dying. I'm not Mother Teresa."

"What is this project about? What have you been writing about?"

I take a deep breath. I'm enjoying my anger, savoring it. What a familiar place this is—I do this all the time with Chris and even with Lillian. I take a shaky breath and slowly answer her, "Listening, waiting, seeing, believing, accepting, unfolding."

"Don't you see, it's been under your nose the entire time. You've been writing about faith."

Faith. The word made my stomach fly into my throat, as it does when I swing with Lilly on the school swings. It sounded so Christian. I didn't hear my Buddhist friends talking about faith.

Yet it also sounded like a concept that I was ripe for. I've been hiding in aisle eight of the spiritual supermarket. A spiritual seeker since the tender age of eleven, when I stole my sister's copy of *Be Here Now* by Ram Dass and began meditating and doing yoga on my own, I was good at aspiring, excellent at searching. I was not so good at settling down. Whether it was the Baptist church at twelve, the Buddhist temple at twenty-two, my goddess circle at twenty-eight, or the Unitarian church at thirty-three, I lasted for a few months or years and then I drifted away, made uneasy by the question "Can Jesus really get me a new bike if I pray for it?" Or the question CQ was pushing me against: "What do I believe?" The Unitarians, who pointedly don't ask this question, lost me simply by not asking.

CQ walks to the pinnacle of the roof and begins a series of yoga sun salutations. Defying the laws of gravity, her crown stays on as she bends down, then swoops up. Big Bird does yoga. "I'm not asking you to say the Nicene Creed. I'm not even asking you what you believe. I'm asking you to have faith."

"What's the difference?" I snap. I still haven't gotten used to her reading my mind.

"Allow me to paraphrase my late friend, the Zen philosopher Alan Watts. I choose Watts to show you Buddhists do think about faith. Watts said that belief is the demand that the truth is what you would 'lief' or wish, while faith is an unqualified yes to the truth, however hard or unflattering that truth might be. Faith has no preconceptions; she plunges into the unknown, a diver on the cliffs above Malta. Belief clings, faith lets go." CQ meets my eye.

I swallow. I feel like an overinflated tire that has just had a little air let out. I feel both good and hollow. I feel my self-importance and hardness soften a little, evaporate on the hot roof.

I don't need to believe to have faith.

I didn't need to *believe*. What a concept. In the heat shimmering off the roof, I saw for the first time how tangled, how stuck, I was in the clash between belief and faith, between the visible and the invisible. I had been looking for ways to move the unseen into the seen. I thought the way to do that was concrete knowledge. I wanted to construct a sure way to define and hold my spiritual life: "Here is what I believe. Here is my research. These highly intellectual people agree with me." The way I saw it, I couldn't have faith because I hadn't done enough research. Venture any further and Harold Bloom, my personal inner critic, would descend in all his tumescent glory to demand how could I be so uninformed? How dare I even utter the word "faith" or speak of larger energies or God until I have read every book ever written, and all unpublished theses too, on every religion, belief system, myth, god, and goddess since the beginning of humanity, and please don't neglect quantum physics, chaos theory, and morph fields (that last part would be from Ken Wilbur, my hip inner intellectual). Without such preparation, I'd soon be sending my life savings to Jan, hostess of the 700 Club, so she could buy more mascara. I'll start walking door to door with copies of the *Watchtower* under my arm, certain that I have the only guaranteed way to snag a good seat in heaven.

To me, believing had always meant making bargains, as in "That went perfectly, everything fell right into place, it must have been orchestrated by a God who loves me." Then, when something went wrong, in my life or in the world, I plunged into disheartenment and hopelessness, declaring there was no Divine Intelligence, no larger energies, and no point to life. I would hide under the covers, clutching my despair, overwhelmed and stunned.

More than stunned—frightened. No, terrified. Terrified to let God know me, to let the invisible into my life. It felt like taking my clothes off in a department store under those spiteful fluorescent lights, trying on a bikini (that alone makes me sob). Suddenly the door is yanked open and every woman I ever felt inferior to, starting in the Murray Middle School locker room, is staring at me. That kind of total exposure of who I am was what I feared if I start believing in a higher power. No, it was worse than that. God would see my terrible rages when I yelled so loud that my throat ached. When I threw things. She would see my greed, my smallness, my desire to hide from all that is painful and harsh. She would see how I *thought* about volunteering at the nursing home while the phone number yellowed and curled on my bulletin board.

Have faith and I wouldn't be able to hide under the covers anymore.

It comforted me slightly that my truly devout friend Mary had her fears of God too. This is what she said in a chapel address she gave during her time at a Christian seminary:

What does it mean to love God? How do we do it? For me, there's always been a serious obstacle: I'm scared of God.

When I was a kid, I guess I heard too many scary missionary stories. I was always afraid God would send me to Timbuktu if I let him take hold of me. The very word "Timbuktu" struck terror into my heart for decades. Of course, once God really gets hold of you, Timbuktu starts looking good. It did for me.

Then I was afraid of being weird, that being a Christian would mean I'd be odd. But the older I get, the more I believe eccentricity is good. There is no bondage like the bondage of going for normalcy, because no one knows what it is. If I told you in the most self-serving terms possible why I'm Christian, I'd have to say I'm in it for the freedom. I can't think of anything more freeing than living clear that it's only God's opinion of me that matters.

Which is interesting, because the truth is, my opinion of God is not always so good. In fact, here's where my fear of God really shows.

I'm afraid I'll have to protect him. I'm afraid he hasn't really been keeping up with advances in science. I'm afraid philosophy has passed him by. I'm afraid his hermeneutics are outdated.

But essentially, you can't love God, you can't know God, if you're afraid your questions will put him on the spot. The problem here is not with God—it's mine. It's my fear.

Freedom and questions. No bondage like the bondage of normalcy. And I would add the bondage of comfort, the comfort of hiding in my little boxes of intellectual knowledge.

"Surrender, Jennifer. That's your ticket, surrender."

I look at CQ, half expecting her to be riding a broom and spelling out the words "Surrender, Jennifer" across the cloudless sky. But she's still sitting near me. Once again, not going anywhere.

"You keep asking me to surrender. I hate it. It feels so submissive to me. It makes my skin crawl. I'm struggling to value my opinions, my experience, to trust my inner voice. Why would I want to give that all up?" I stand up, then sit down, twist my neck from side to side.

"Why do you assume God wants you to give that up? Hasn't the discipline of listening taught you anything, hasn't it led you closer both to yourself and to the larger energies? Why do you persist in seeing the Divine in such a dualist way? You tell Lilly that the Divine is inside her and inside everything, but you exempt yourself from that truth," CQ challenges me.

"I thought if I didn't know what I believed *in,* I couldn't have faith. I thought if I couldn't surrender, I couldn't believe." I'm trying hard to keep the whine out of my voice.

"You do have to surrender. It is a matter of what you surrender." CQ folds her hands into a prayer position and bows.

Living the Questions

30

WHAT ARE MY TWO OR THREE GREATEST STRESS POINTS RIGHT NOW—
THE PEOPLE, PLACES, AND THINGS THAT MAKE ME GRIND MY TEETH
OR SPIN INTO URGENCY MODE?

Keep it simple and focus on the points that are most important to you, not what others would name important. These may be the same stresses or discomforts you've been working on for the entire book, or they may be new ones that relate to your upcoming week.

HOW COULD FAITH HELP ME WITH THESE STRESSES AND DISCOMFORTS?
WHAT WOULD IT LOOK LIKE IF I CLEARLY SAW MYSELF TRUSTING
IN THE POWER OF MY INTENTION AND MY CONNECTION
TO THE DIVINE INTELLIGENCE?

It may be difficult to name how faith could help. Perhaps putting down your pen and moving to music will help? Imagine in metaphors instead of linear, concrete words.

WHAT ONE PERSON IN MY LIFE HAVEN'T I BEEN FEELING
COMPLETELY COMFORTABLE WITH?

It may be the same person of whom you asked this question before. It may be someone new or even surprising. Don't push the knowledge away. Breathe into it.

WHAT DO I KNOW IN MY HEART IS NEEDED TO BRING THIS RELATIONSHIP
INTO A MORE HONEST AND BALANCED PLACE?

Avoid things like "Grovel at their feet" and "Buy them a ticket to Kauai." Stick to small, heartfelt but not necessarily easy actions.

Faith Too

"Surrender like the fourteenth-century Japanese potter who couldn't get his glazes right until he walked into the kiln and became the glaze." CQ throws her arms out wide. "Like the novice who comes to her abbess, whining, 'I'm doing everything right: I'm praying, I'm scourging myself, I'm studying my Bible, but nothing is happening.' And the abbess spreads her arms and says, 'Why not try turning into fire?' You are being asked to let go and plunge *without* knowing, without choosing, and without staying in your head, where you have, I will very politely point out, been most of your life."

"I like being one giant head, floating around. It's so clean." I imagine myself as Snoopy's Great Pumpkin, finally arriving in time for Halloween.

"You have to understand that faith is not something you can bottle and sell, not a way to mollify your fears or remove your suffering. You don't get to wear henna tattoos or make a music video in your antique sari or become a popular spiritual teacher who lectures to thousands," CQ says. "You don't get to make bargains with God; that's confusing getting what you want with surrendering to the Divine. You've slipped into thinking that if you contemplate your questions, write in your gratitude journal, meditate, avoid judgmental thoughts, and recycle religiously, you will be blessed with everything you've ever wanted and that this or something better will now happen for the greater good of all concerned. That is not faith; that is plea-bargaining."

"I'm good at plea-bargaining."

CQ is not laughing at my lame attempts to sidestep her questioning. I stretch my legs and reach for my toes, avoiding her probing gaze. She wants me to accept all this faith stuff, this suspicious surrendering stuff, without excessive whining, berating of innocent bystanders (especially the one I'm married to), or holding back and making bargains?

"You do know that you are asking an awful lot," I say.

"You're the one who invited me," she shoots back. Then reaching out to stroke my arm with an immense tenderness that billows throughout my body, she says, "You can do this."

Despair licks my ankles, the familiar urge to go downstairs and devour something sugary. Self-pity beckons, as cozy as my flannel pajamas. I thought I was doing so well, making such progress. All I along I wasn't getting it. I was, once again, better at teaching it than *breathing* it. I scuttle downstairs, toward the kitchen.

CQ intercepts me. "The creative moment is *now.* Surrender into the moment. That is faith. Self-pity is a great drinking buddy, but all he ever created were doodles on soggy cocktail napkins." Before I can mewl, CQ puts on a CD of sinuous, scorching music, and starts to jeté and undulate (hard to do at the same time), a dream figure, whirling around my living room, crowned and bejeweled. All I want to do is disappear into the kitchen and rendezvous with a large bag of cookies. Still, something in me has the energy to follow her.

CQ circles around me, her big feet pounding my wood floors, her voice a purr. "Ask yourself, *without* denying that you crave the cookie, *without* denying that you want to cuddle up with Mr. Self-Pity, without beating yourself up, 'What am I connected to?' But don't answer it with your mind. Don't even expect an answer. You aren't remotely interested in knowing the answer. You wouldn't take an answer even if it came with thin thighs, $10 million, and Antonio Banderas. You long for the question, every molecule of your self longs to experience the mystery, 'What am I connected to?'"

I watch my feet move up and down, back and forth. I'm connected to the floor. I'm not connected to the floor. I want to be connected to food. To the familiar. CQ brushes against me. I'm connected to her. But she doesn't exist. Or is she more real than me? I'm connected to this house, my possessions. I move around the room, touching my couch, my table, the books, pictures of my family. I'm connected, I'm tethered, I exist. . . .

I'm still in my head. CQ whirls by. "There isn't an answer. You don't have to have a blinding epiphany. Feel the longing, enter it. This is surrender, leaping into God without knowing."

As Ms. Amazon lifts the chairs and couch out of our way, clearing a larger dance space, as the music resonates through me, digeradoos, bird chirps, snaking drums, I give myself to it. Give myself over. I don't have to do anything. I don't have to know. Where are you, God?

In that moment, brief and translucent, I slip my hand into faith's. I feel myself connect.

IF I COULD DO OR BE OR FEEL ANYTHING IN THE COMING DAYS, WHAT WOULD IT BE?

In love with myself
In union with the universe
Bursting with creative energy
Eating exactly what my body needs
Singing
Retreating

Fulfilling a wish via effort and
    determination
Forgiving myself
Celebrating myself
Connecting with someone I love
Making love to my potential
Or ____

AM I WILLING TO TRY? CAN I GIVE MYSELF AT LEAST A TASTE OF WHATEVER IT IS I'VE DREAMED UP?

CQ asks gently, "What is in your way? You don't have to name it, but can you sense its molten, moving, core? How will you dodge around it, leap over it, incorporate its heat? Use your intention to help you."

IN THE DAYS AHEAD, HOW CAN I MAKE A COMMITMENT TO BE DEEPLY RESPONSIBLE FOR MY OWN COMFORT? HOW MIGHT I CHANGE MY ENVIRONMENT, CHANGE MY ATTITUDE ABOUT SOMETHING THAT IS BOTHERING ME, OR RELEASE TENSION IN MY BODY?

Notice what happens when you take responsibility for your comfort—how does your day shift?

WHO AND WHAT DO I FEEL GRATITUDE FOR? HOW COULD I EXPRESS THAT GRATITUDE TO A PERSON OR TO THE DIVINE?

Think offering, ritual, gift. Think realistic, doable, self-loving, giving from your abundance.

Listening to the World

"**N**othing I had planned, organized, or orchestrated for groups I had lead out of my intense spiritual need had gotten me to that place of deepest nurturing," Marcie said. "So much personal energy goes into finding a reason or shape for something so that it may be expressed or shared with others. The most freeing thing is to simply value hearing the wind in the trees. It is so relieving. Who knows where the wind comes from? When you can focus on the signature of the Divine, you are able to listen from both within and without. To do that is the most nurturing and the most freeing thing. To remove the effort of our personal energy long enough to listen, to both inner and outer Nature at the same time." When Marcie told me this about her spiritual life being completely remolded partly because she shifted to listening not only to her interior world but to the exterior world as well, I recalled a spiritual shift that had taken place in me when I was pregnant with Lilly. During my almost daily walks up Rattlesnake Canyon, I had been overtaken with and deeply comforted by a very clear and real sense that everything around me was awake and alive. I remember staring down at a stratified rock that ran across the trail and thinking—no, not thinking, *experiencing*—that rock as the backbone of the world.

It is this experience that we need to add to our listening. We must each find ways to notice, to tune in to and learn what the world outside our skin is trying to teach us. We have to lift our heads up and pay attention to what is being offered. We have to find out how we can live in wonder at our interconnectedness.

In his astonishing book *The Spell of the Sensuous,* David Abram notes, "The most sophisticated definition of 'magic' that now circulates through the American counterculture is 'the ability or power to alter one's consciousness at will.' No mention is made of any *reason* for altering one's consciousness." In tribal cultures, "magic" means being able to experience your consciousness as simply one form of awareness among many others. Abram notes that shamans and traditional magicians cultivate an ability to shift out of everyday consciousness so that they can contact and learn from the other forms of life. The shaman readily slips out of such limiting boundaries as social customs, taboos, and language in order to enter a state of "heightened receptivity to the meaningful solicitations—songs, cries, gestures—of the larger, more-than-human field." Or as Marcie put it, "The woodpecker outside my window just stopped pecking, turned, and looked at me as I told you this story of learning to listen within and without. There's something valuable there. I'm going to listen to that."

There is a moment in each of our lives when we gain enough strength, confidence, and trust in our inner process to begin listening to the greater whole. It may be that you have always listened but now you are able to do so in a way that informs your life as much (or almost as much) as your inner work. The inner and the outer merge. Many cultures believe our individual soul extends beyond the boundaries of our body. We know that matter is not solid or separate. When we remember this, it no longer feels strange to receive reassurance and guidance from outside our own consciousness. We discover that when the world is approached with trust, it offers us friendship. When we wait and ruminate, we find the rhythm of the universe.

Sometimes a bolt of synchronicity startles you into lifting up your head, a meaningful coincidence envelopes you with a clear message: there is something moving through you, inspiring you, egging you on toward wholeness. Perhaps a prayer is answered in such a clear way that you are awed by the presence of God. Or you spend the night watching the stars and the stars watch you right back. A miracle blossoms. Perhaps you consult the I Ching or the tarot, or an experienced and gifted astrologer reads your chart. Dianne Skafte in *Listening to the Oracle* notes that thousands of methods have been used in numerous cultures to obtain answers to questions or to see into the deeper meaning of issues. We are either a loony bin of humans, cracking agates on hot surfaces and examining pigs' entrails for messages, or we know that guidance and illumination are available from sources beyond ourselves. Dianne writes that as she delved deeper into researching oracles she "no longer felt marooned in a barren world from which signs and wonders had fled. I knew now that the oracular 'others' were with us and had never departed. The task ahead, I realized, was to start *remembering*." Perhaps what I'm getting at is what

Jung meant when he said, "Is he or she related to something infinite or not?" But I had always conceived of his question in terms of believing, not as perceiving and being open to the whole.

Once we know and love ourselves intimately, we can teeter on the razor's edge between creating our lives and letting our lives create us. We can surrender in ways that allow us to constantly learn from being a tiny fraction of the whole, from being deeply interconnected. We can balance our absorption in our interior world with acknowledgment and homage to the visible and invisible powers around us. "We begin to realize ours are not the only questions. While we are questioning, we are also *being* questioned," notes Maria Harris in *Dance of the Spirit*. Who is questioning you? Who is speaking to you? What are they trying to tell you?

It is not the momentous encounters during times of transition or crises I'm so attracted to, although these are often our wake-up call. It is the daily feeling of being connected and of listening for help, sometimes in the form of a caress, sometimes in the form of more overt guidance, that we can weave into our lives. We need an experience of the Divine that is big enough to handle our deeply ingrained patterns of self-doubt, to encompass the loopy farrago that life brings, to penetrate our loneliness. We must practice, in our own way (not learned from a weekend seminar in spirituality but through our own experience and experimentation), the essence of the skills a shaman uses in a traditional culture. We must shift out of our everyday consciousness and into the great web, and wait there, listening.

When I get up in the morning, I can invite the visible and invisible into my experience by taking my tea to the oak tree at the back of my yard and pouring a little offering to it, then sitting down and watching the world. I may do this watching in the context of a question like "How can I become the person I am meant to be?" I may see what the sky, the leaves, the gopher, the budding corn, has to say in answer. I may, at times, be able to expand to another perspective, where I don't do the asking, I let the world ask me. Or I may put no concept on it. I may simply sit, aware that I and the yard are strumming and unfolding together. I lift up my head and take in information from the world.

I do my offering to physically feel I am not alone. If I am to continue my practice of listening, this is what I *need:* to be addressed in an intimate, helpful way by something wiser than myself, to have my cheek nuzzled by a brush of otherness. I will not persevere, I did not persevere in the past, by relying solely on my personal resources day after day.

All we have to do, all we can do, is pay attention and value these experiences of the "other" that we perceive. This doesn't mean romanticize them or become someone who can't buy bananas without checking the tarot cards. You don't invite a stranger you met at the store in a purple shirt to stay with you because last night you had a dream about a man in a purple shirt. We must not forget the union of opposites: the importance of relation married to rightness of action, being to doing, magic allied with science, logic enraptured with intuition.

We learn to trust that the hunger we feel for union is not about looking for answers outside of ourselves, is not about looking for an excuse to hide behind doctrine and dogma. It is a willingness to face our despair and existential aloneness, and still bound into the icy, high breakers, saying, "I will go on, I will feel, I will connect," at the same time we watch for who and what meets us in the ocean.

WHAT IS THE ONE THING I NEED MORE OF IN MY LIFE RIGHT NOW?

Beauty
Respect
Organization
Spontaneity
Stamina
Community
Direction

Commitment
Patience with myself
Trust
Discipline
Accessories (just kidding)
Fill in the blank: ____

Pick the *one* thing you *need* most.

WHAT MODEST STEPS AM I WILLING TO TAKE
TO GET MORE ____ IN MY LIFE?

HOW CAN I SUPPORT MY PRICELESS SELF?

MUSICALLY: Take piano, violin, accordion lessons, hang wind chimes outside your bedroom window, sit still and listen to a Bach concerto . . .

ECSTATICALLY: Invite openness, tenderness, melting, daring into your heart; lick honey off your fingers; feed someone grapes; pray as you've never prayed before; make love to a tree . . .

CONNECTING WITH OTHERS: Spur-of-the-moment potluck with neighbors, inviting a few of your fellow art class students to tea, looking a homeless woman in the eyes when you give her change . . .

Note from CQ: *"This question business can be astoundingly hard work; you can work yourself to the bone. I hope, I just hope, you are taking plenty of breaks, sipping a little of my soup, giving yourself a healthy number of pats on your strong back."*

Receiving

One of the reasons it can be hard to maintain our vision over the long haul is that it is so difficult for us to receive. This is one of our central obstacles. We are so incredibly good at giving to and doing for others. We are getting much better at giving to ourselves. But there is *major* room for improvement in the realm of receiving, a realm that encompasses letting in, letting go, and asking for help.

A friend borrowed money from me for two weeks. She tried to pay me interest. I said, "I'll kill you if you pay me interest." Pat offers to go to the hospital with a friend who is alone with her sick baby. "I'll kill you if you go to the hospital without me," Pat jokes. We were both joking, but our jokes reveal how hard it is to convince our friends to let us help them and perhaps how badly we want to help.

After help is received, how quickly we move to even the score, to say thank you. Doing two small favors for a neighbor one day resulted in Amy receiving a luxurious bouquet of roses early the next morning. Anita's friend Sherry was suffering terribly from shingles. Anita offered to take Sherry's son for a few afternoons. The day of the first play date, Sherry called, "Now, if you need to change plans, that's okay." A friend of mine came to pick up her daughter and we invited her to stay for dinner. Her husband was out of town, it was six o'clock, and the power was out at her house. We almost had to force her to sit at the table, and she must have said thanks at least ten times.

Why do we do refuse to receive or to ask for help? There are probably billions of reasons, personal and universal. Here are a few I've unearthed:

❋ The institution of womanhood, especially motherhood, is charged with the frightening implication that to be a good woman we must be selfless, utterly giving at all times, or we are negligent and inadequate. We have been taught to give to others, to nurture others first. Many of us have founded our very identities on this belief.

❋ We have fought hard for our independence. Receiving encroaches on it, or at least seems to in a hierarchical world, whispering, "Maybe you aren't as capable as we thought."

❋ We may secretly believe that healthy, together women don't need help: "It's okay for someone else to ask for help, but not me."

❋ Receiving support touches on our fear of intimacy, indebtedness, and obligation and enmeshes us in community. It is less complicated, cleaner, to go it alone.

❋ We may worry that will we grow to like the kindness or generosity being shown us and at that very moment, it will be taken away.

In my workshops, I have participants split into two groups. One group sits while the other group stands behind them. Each woman who is standing whispers an affirmation into the ear of the woman sitting in front of her. She whispers the affirmation as an "I" statement (the woman sitting down might hear "I can be kind to myself" or "I can find time to play the piano" or "Health is my birthright and I can create it") and moves around the circle, repeating it to each woman. After everyone has heard these divine, warm little whispers (I pass out mints before the circle), everyone takes a breath. Then the women standing sit and the seated women stand, and we repeat the process. This ritual leaves most of the women crying, and often melts the one or two women who have been listening to me with arms folded over their chests and a dismissive look in their eyes.

Why? Because women hear kind things said in a female voice. Most of us talk to ourselves so harshly, we wouldn't talk to a dog with mange the way we talk to ourselves. Hearing each woman's hopes and yearnings tells us we are not alone in our attempts to be kind to ourselves. That is so affirming. Finally, we are put in the receiving mode for a few cherished moments, not having to *give* anything, just *receive*. I tell the women sitting down, "You have the hardest job of all. You have to close your eyes, breathe, and receive. Let the words in."

Talking to ourselves kindly eases receiving. As does remembering how good it feels when we help someone else. When my neighbors, the Smiths, needed some pasta for their dinner, I made them swear not to replace it the next day. It felt so good to give them that little gift. Who are we to stop others from experiencing that satisfying feeling of helping by hastily evening the score or by never asking for help in the first place?

We have to leap and have faith that we are worthy to receive the gift. We have to leap and have faith as we open to the feelings receiving brings. We must leap and hope others are trustworthy. The only way this is going to happen is . . . yes, by leaping, and by practicing awareness. And it can be helpful to examine our relationship to receiving.

* Where do we need to ask for help?
* Where do we need to step back and see what help appears?
* Where are we giving to others but not what they really want or need?
* How can we give more generously, without feeling that we are creating a sense of burden, debt, or obligation? (Too often I have not asked this question of women for fear of sending them back over the edge into endless penance. Yet as emerging Comfort Queens, we are strong enough to ask this question too.)
* How or who have we asked for help in the past? Did it work or not? Who are we asking too much of?

Yet I don't want to oversimplify the perils of asking for help or to imply that just because you ask, you will receive. "Learning to know what we want and then to honestly ask for it is a monumental achievement," Elizabeth Lesser notes in *The New American Spirituality.* "But so is learning to gracefully accept all that is given and taken away."

Different styles of giving and receiving conflict, as do expectations, and adding the burden of life can make it all but impossible to give or receive help. After Sherry got well, Sherry and Anita had a distressing fight. Sherry felt that Anita hadn't offered her enough care and help while she was sick, and Anita felt that every time she tried to help, Sherry had refused her offer or been unwilling to state what she wanted: "Sherry thought I should know her well enough to know what she needed without her having to ask." Anita frowned. "I'm not good at thinking of ways to nurture people. I hate guessing what people want, and I'm overwhelmed in my own life right now. I just couldn't help her the way she needed." How fraught with difficulty giving and receiving can be!

Grace happens when we hook up with someone who can give to us in a way we can appreciate and be open to. Marcie had taught me this on my summer visit. Her hospitality was so natural and unfussy. Not once did she hover, apologize for the state of her home, or ask me if I needed anything. She had faith in me to ask for what I needed and to take care of myself. Having been raised in a somewhat southern tradition, where a woman is doing her job if she hovers over her guest, I found Marcie's approach downright revolutionary. As soon as I got home, I tried not hovering over my friend Mary, who was staying with us for the night. I found I could focus on *her* instead of nervously jumping up to impress her with my care.

Lest this begin to sound like *Hints from Heloise,* I'll inject another truthful but melancholy note. Being in the pit for so long and watching my friend Mina suffer through her even longer pit tenure had taught me that when we are down for a long time, we must spread our misery around. You can only call so many times and hear the depressed voice droopily muttering, "No, really, I'm fine." As one friend said to me during my pit tenure, "I've never had a friend who was so gloomy." Part of me wanted to sock her in the solar plexus; the other part of me understood completely because I've been on the receiving end of depressed friends. When we are down for a long time, we have to adjust our expectations of what others are capable of giving to us, and we must be sure we are sharing a portion of our pain with the Divine. He/She/It can handle it.

My parents always said, "Don't be beholden to anyone. Neither a borrower nor a lender be." Are we afraid that by asking for help or allowing others to help us we will be taken advantage of, put in a powerless position? That seems reasonable. People do take advantage. Many of us have burned out on giving to others. "Each woman needs her very own Comfort Queen to lay a restraining hand on her arm and say, 'Whoa there, girl, slow down. That's just about enough giving.'" I jerk my hands away from my computer keyboard. It's typing without me. I look around for CQ and see that the speakers on either side of my monitor are displaying twin smiles. "Hello, CQ, how are you?" I type back.

She types: "You've been able to receive me, to let me in."

I answer, "In case you've forgotten, that's because you're imaginary. What threat are you to me? Real receiving is what happens in community, and that scares the hell out of me. It's messy, scary, intimate stuff, and it makes me feel interconnected, vulnerable, and needy. I think us white western raised-in-the-suburb types don't do well with community or receiving. That's why we worship our self-contained cars and our neatly delineated yards."

CQ types quickly. I watch the keyboard, fascinated. I wonder briefly if I can persuade her to write the rest of the book. "I'm just as messy, scary and intimate as your other communities," she writes. "If you haven't seen that yet, you will." This makes me suck my breath in nervously. After a moment, CQ adds, "You crave community and you need it to survive. Everybody needs to belong."

I answer. "Needing it and doing it are two different things. Doing community, letting real receiving in, means allowing others to *see* us, without our *i*'s dotted and our makeup on."

"You've got to be willing to unmask your heart. You've got to be willing to let others see your ugly side. That's what most people aren't good at: witnessing each other's ugly side and still sticking around. Too many of you run away too easily," CQ types.

"How do I know *you* will stick around?" I type back, then pause, surprised at what I've written.

The keyboard is motionless for a long moment. I'm about to type something lame like "Oh, I know you'll stick around," when she answers me.

"I'll be here as long as you don't fail yourself. Your inner world will sustain you when community fails you and you fail community, *if* you build your life from the inside out and *if* you let yourself receive." Another pause. I close my eyes and breathe in her words. Then the keys start clicking again. "Consider this: What if God is speaking to you, caring for all of you, through the arms of your friends and neighbors? What if by refusing to receive you are blocking Divine Love, the Divine Hello? If you don't believe that you can, know this much is true: You are blocking love and caring from another human when you refuse to receive or ask. You are poorer for it, and you make your life a lot harder than it has to be. Everybody has abundances. Why do you deny yours?"

I rock back and forth in my desk chair, considering her words.

"It's awful cramped in here, so I'm just going to say one more thing before I push on. In the end, my dear, you have no choice. You cannot do it alone."

The keys fall silent. I'm starting to know when CQ's present and when she's—*whoosh!*—gone. I wonder where she goes. I get up to stretch, look out the window.

My girlfriend pulls into the driveway. I had forgotten she was coming over to borrow an outfit for a wedding this coming weekend. She knocks, comes inside, and finds me in my office. She smiles at me quizzically. "You okay?"

"Can I have a hug?"

Just let that love in, Jennifer, let it in.

Before I head downstairs to rummage in my closet with her, I write, "Receiving allows us to sustain the unfolding of our lives. Without it, we are sunk."

WHAT HAVE I ALLOWED MYSELF TO RECEIVE IN THE LAST FEW DAYS?

A moment of grace, eye contact with a stranger, the relief of getting a job done?

WHAT DO I WISH I HAD LET MYSELF RECEIVE?

"Can you hear me when I say, 'You divine creation. Can you *see* how marvelous you are? Why not delight in being a work in progress?" CQ sends a cool swirl of rose- and grapefruit-scented praise around your body and soul. Breathe it in.

WHAT ONE INSIGHT AM I FOLDING INTO MY LIFE THESE DAYS? AM I READY FOR A NEW ONE? DO I NEED TO REVAMP THE ONE I'VE BEEN WORKING ON OR SIMPLY KEEP MOVING AHEAD IN MODEST STEPS?

What happens if you connect your insight with your intention?

HOW PRESENT IS SHADOW COMFORT IN MY LIFE THESE DAYS?

Remember, the more change is happening, the more the same old stuff comes roaring back into our face. You could look upon bouts of shadow comfort or other behavior as a setback but instead trust that these moments are new opportunities to release an old way of being and choose the path of learning and self-love. When I started seeing each time I ate food that was bad for me not as indictment of my character but as an opportunity to learn and love myself, things shifted.

HOW HUNGRY ARE MY TIME MONSTERS?

In the Green River in Utah, there live lots of large catfish. These whiskery devils make nasty little gummy noises as their mouths poke through the surface. Time monsters and these catfish resemble each other.

Inmates and Intimates

Many of us have made huge progress reestablishing the bonds of female friendship. I feel almost as committed to my friendships and my women's group as I do to my marriage.

Our friendships help us create our lives, reflecting back to us what we can become and supporting us when we stumble in our stretching. Our male-female relationships can do the same, but often they do this in a more unsettling and contentious manner (a polite understatement if there ever was one). The territory where our fierce desire meets a beloved's fierce desire, resistance, or indifference is the place where, second only to raising a child and caring for an elderly parent, many of us flounder.

As one woman who was quoted by Sherry Ruth Anderson and Patricia Hopkins in *The Feminine Face of God* said of her nearly forty-year marriage, "Only recently have I begun to realize how subtly and expertly I've designed my life to stay within the security of his love." For years, I've been haunted by what Anderson and Hopkins discovered: "Although all but three of the women we interviewed had been married at least once, over seventy percent of the marriages had ended in divorce, and fewer than a third of the women were married or living in committed relationships at the time we spoke to them.... In our male-dominated culture, what happens when women no longer need or want to defer to men? What happens when we no longer automatically modulate our personalities or reorder our priorities to accommodate our husband or lover? Does the glue that holds male-female relationships together break down? The immediate answer, in terms of our research, is yes."

When we create our lives, when we practice listening, at some point we become *incapable* of deferring or modulating our personalities to accommodate a husband or a lover or, for that matter, a friend, because in doing so we will betray the very path we have been trying so hard to perceive. If the relationship model most of us have been raised with includes deference, even in very subtle ways, how do we have a relationship with a man? How do we learn from women who followed their unfolding paths and ended up alone, and didn't want to, especially when children were involved?

I have never believed that we must be in partnership to be whole. I understand my friends who love living alone, and of course I sometimes envy them. Yet for those of us who are in relationships, it is a tremendous, urgent question: how to stay in the relationship while remaining true to our emerging selves?

I thought we had answered that question in the very beginning of our marriage. I thought I was being true to myself and Chris to himself. I certainly wasn't deferring to Chris. I thought we had created an equal partnership where we both could flourish.

Yet what has become clear in the last two years is that all we've really done is reverse the roles. Chris was adjusting to me instead of us adjusting to each other. Chris has met my strident need for equality at the price of his own sense of mastery and even, to a small degree, his male identity. Because Chris and I connect with life through our work, there is much at stake. Work isn't a career or a job to us; it's the central way, besides parenting, that we experience meaning. We both struggle to balance being parents, creative people, and breadwinners, but my work has edged out Chris's passion because I make more money.

Many issues are intertwined here. The cultural edict that the breadwinner in the relationship is more important is certainly one example. She or he is entitled to sleep in after a deadline is met, to take a bike ride after a long day, to approach parenting as an extracurricular activity. Then there is the reality that we may find meaning in our work, but one of has to make enough money to pay the bills. Yet what I've discovered is that these are surface concerns. Underneath, the central issue is my fear, which I have dressed up in feminism to hide from. My fear: that my work is not real and therefore I must protect it at all costs. Similar to my fear of surrender, which has hindered my religious life, I am afraid to surrender to Chris's needs because then I would not be able to pursue my passion. Not that he would stop me but that I would stop myself. Being a creative person has always felt so tenuous to me. Was I really a writer? Translation: was I really an adult, responsible for and *capable* of creating my life? Could I really stay connected to the meaning of my life without my books being published? When someone interrupted me by calling in the middle of the day (as if I had to answer the phone) or by inviting me to lunch, I would often become angry, and would complain to Chris, "Don't they think I work?" Thou dost protest too much.

I used my feminism to straitjacket our relationship, cutting off the flow and constant adjustment that *is* marriage, using my legitimate demand for equality to hide from the greater emotional and spiritual challenge of discerning when to be receptive and when to stand my ground, refusing to either dominate or depend. And yet, even this description doesn't say it all. In the beginning of our marriage, I didn't demand equality because of my fear that I wasn't in charge of my life. I demanded equality because I knew if I didn't, it wouldn't happen. Our problems started when my insistence became snarled with my making more money than Chris, with the question of who parents when, and with my fear of being taken seriously.

I have faith that our guardian angels colluded to get us together or, on a less woo-woo level, we are together to learn from each other much that is essential for our growth to wholeness. Therefore I am learning to have faith that our work together is as essential for the unfolding of my path as anything else. In the past, I have reinforced our situation by subtly believing that what I'm doing alone in my inner world is more central to my life's development than the alchemy that happens when two people choose a conscious marriage. I had to do what Sheila, whom I quoted earlier, had done, when she decided, "Self-nurturing wasn't going to be a treat but a way of life. I had to shift from doing it alone to making it part of my relationships." I had to connect with my creative source and strengthen myself *through* my relationship, instead of only outside of it. This could sound like dangerous backsliding to the days when women got their creative fulfillment through their men, and men accessed their emotional life through women. But there were several important differences. I had had and *still had* my own connection to my creative source. Now I was sensing how to use that place as a launching pad to true give-and-take within my marriage. I now knew I was good enough, I was capable of creating my life, so I no longer had to jealously guard myself. I could sacrifice myself for the greater good of the relationship. I kept wanting to find the right answer or to know what was *fair*. But there is no right answer, except that it isn't mine and yours; it is mine, yours, and ours.

WHERE AM I PINCHING OR TWISTING MY LIFE'S SHAPE TO FIT SOMEONE ELSE'S?

Parents, boss, sister, brother, friend, church, partner in love, partner in business?

WHERE AM I PINCHING SOMEONE ELSE'S LIFE TO FIT MINE?

Same list of suspects.

WHAT PURPOSE IS THIS PINCHING SERVING?

CQ whistles. "Take it easy on this one, slow and easy. Peer a little into why you are pinching or being pinched. It may be a choice. It may be necessary. All I'm asking for is a little gentle awareness."

WHAT YEARNINGS AM I GIVING ROOM TO GROW? HOW IS MY INTENTION HELPING THAT YEARNING TO BLOOM?

Money, Love, and Creating a Life

Here's another hard-won lesson: whoever controls the most economic power in the relationship has the greater obligation to make sure his or her fierce desire doesn't overrun the other person's. We live in a world that values money over everything else, no matter how many press conferences we hold to pontificate about family values. The equation is simple, devastating, and all-pervasive: I make more money, so my time is more valuable. If we are to truly co-create, we must work diligently to keep this mind-set out of our intimate relationships.

On the other hand, if you don't hold the economic key, you have to be sure you aren't subtly feeding the belief that your time is less valuable by accepting less personal time. You have to accept the responsibility to say, "My life's path matters as much as yours, even if right now that path seems to be quiet and slow and is making little or no money." One person trades her time for money and another person trades his caring for the children, caring for our mother, building our house, or managing our investments. That time is traded equally. And the time left when those work hours are over is also divided fairly.

That's great. But what happens when one partner's job takes all his or her time and there is no free time left to divide? Pamela loves her husband, loves her kids, juggles two jobs, and almost never sees her husband because of the demands of his job. She feels resentful, overwhelmed, and has no idea what to do. "I don't want to leave the guy because he works all the time, but this is not the way I want my life to be," she says. Pamela has a fierce desire to have more time to herself and for her children. But her husband's job precludes that.

Or consider Petra. She worked at a high-powered, stressful job she did not enjoy while raising her daughter alone. When her daughter was eight, Petra remarried and had a child with her new husband, who also had a successful career. She was elated to quit and became a full-time wife and mom. Now their second child is entering junior high. Her husband has become unhappy with his job. He yearns to do something else but is afraid he will make less money and won't be able to provide for his family in the style to which they have become accustomed (nothing grand, but you know the drill). Petra doesn't want to work outside the home. Her fierce desire is for balance and spiritual growth. Her husband has an emerging fierce desire that could require her to go back to work. His duty is to become clear on what he wants. Her duty is to listen to him and herself. Together they must reject easy answers of "I should do this" or "I shouldn't feel this" and create together what helps them both to develop.

Whose path comes first? How do you fit your passionate life path with economic reality or your mate's need to do things a certain way? If I had easy, concrete answers, I'd be shooting my infomercial right now. I do see, however, several patterns.

- Women too often automatically defer their passion and life's desire.
- Men and women don't inquire fully into what they individually desire.
- Couples don't talk to each other about these gray areas, which allows the proverbial pink elephant to inhabit the living room. It's as if, because of their ego attachment to being the breadwinner, men are afraid to say, "I need you to provide too."
- Meanwhile women often seem unable to say, "You don't matter more just because you make more money."
- When children enter the picture, too often we assume the questions are "Will Mom work or not?" and "Will Mom hurt our child if she works?" instead of "Who works when?" and "How do we create a culture around us that supports families?" We have to graduate from the question of moms working or not and enter into a dialogue about balance and support for moms *and* dads.

We have to learn to embrace sacrifice and take the long view. We may have strong dreams and yet put them off for years so that we can tend our family or support our mate in his or her dream. Great. As long as it is done consciously, as in shared consciousness, and not at the expense of your life's blood. Too often this scenario slides into Mom coming last on everything. Not acceptable.

We chose our relationships. We can unchoose them and walk away, or we can accept that we are here for a reason. The work and compromise we do with our mates is an integral part of our unfolding lives. This stance requires—you guessed it—faith, in ourselves and our partners. Faith that we can create relationships that are fair from the inside out.

WHAT DO I NEED TO DO IN THE COMING DAYS TO SUPPORT THE PERSON I AM BECOMING?

You may not be able to say who you are becoming, or you may feel that who you want to become is such a long shot, why bother? Would CQ give up? "You know the answer to that!" CQ yells from who-knows-where.

WHAT'S HAPPENING WITH MY OBSTACLES TO RELAXATION AND SELF-NURTURING? HAVE THEY CHANGED, DISAPPEARED, GROWN MORE INTENSE, OR SIMPLY STAYED THE SAME?

Read back over this book. Chart what has shifted, notice what has been effective, and perhaps decide on one modest step to take toward continuing to work with these obstacles.

WHAT DO I NEED TO FORGIVE MYSELF FOR? WHAT DO I NEED TO FORGIVE SOMEONE ELSE FOR?

Forgiveness comes on little mouse feet, skitters under the furniture, hides, then lets you glimpse it for a moment before it hides again. But if you are persistent and don't close the door, each time forgiveness will come closer and closer.

WHAT ONE TRANSFORMATIVE, SPINE-TINGLING COMFORT QUEEN THOUGHT CAN I HOLD IN MY HEART AND MIND IN THE COMING DAYS?

Domenica offered me this principle: "I pray and invite help in those moments which feel jarring or overly exciting." Think about your intention—it may inspire a nourishing thought.

Verve Talk

Even More Comfort Queen Stories

We light the candles, sprawl on our respective couches, so very grateful to enter this sanctuary of silence and storytelling. We sit for a while, just listening to our internal stories, absorbing that there is no place else to be but here. Then a woman gently breaks the silence and begins to speak.

"I am hiking with my family in a wilderness area," Barbara tells us. "It is early winter. My six-year-old daughter and I leave my husband to hike to a nearby summit. We start playing, jumping between boulders, and we lose the trail. We are lost. The shadows are growing longer and longer. In perhaps an hour, it will be dusk, and the temperature will start dropping rapidly. We're lost, I think silently. And I have my child with me. As we call for my husband, I'm completely terrified. Yet I force myself to listen. I know that our safety now rests in understanding, not fleeing from this silence I've been making friends with. No matter how

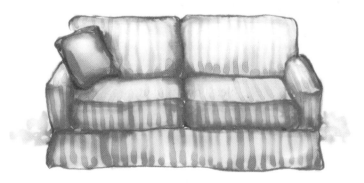

intense my outer turmoil, inwardly I land on the solid soil of my soul. I am learning to listen to it—and trust it—as a guide. Slowly I turn, feeling the wind hit my face. The wind . . . I stand there, letting its silent force swirl into my own silence. Waiting. It is hitting my left cheek. Suddenly I remember: the wind was on my left cheek when we climbed up the trail; I need to turn until it is on my right cheek. When we find our way down the mountain, back to the car, I feel such awe and amazement rising within me. My inner silence found for me the safe route home. I entrusted the safety of myself and my child, for the first time, to the silence within me."

There is no need for words. Someone passes a bottle of mineral water around. Everyone else waits until someone is ready to tell another story.

"I was carrying on about the usual stuff that bothers me at work like not getting enough done, being overwhelmed, general kvetching," Anna says as she arranges the pillows behind her. "I ran outside after a client, to give her something she forgot. The wind was really blowing, and as I was walking back to the house, I noticed that one plant wasn't being whipped around like all the other plants. It really stood out. It was maintaining its place within the whipping wind. I noticed it and it resonated in me: I could do the same thing. In that moment, I recommitted myself to maintaining my sense of calm even as life is going on around me, whether it is children killing children or too much dirty laundry. I was so thankful as I went inside and shut the door."

The wind has been rattling the windows all night and chooses right now to give the French doors a good bang. The women laugh. "It's wind-story night," someone offers.

"I just read a story about the wind," I say. "It's a story from the Sufi teaching tradition from Idries Shah's book *Tales of the Dervishes*. It's about Fatima and it goes like this. Fatima worked for many years with her father, spinning thread into exotic colors. One day her father said to her, 'Fatima, you have worked so hard. Now we must go on a long journey to sell your wares. Perhaps, in the course of this journey, we will find you a handsome and appropriate young man to marry.' So they set off full of hope. Just off the coast of Crete, a terrible storm arose, and the ship was dashed on the rocks. All were drowned except Fatima, who was washed ashore near Alexandria. She was taken in by a family of weavers, who taught her their craft. Within a few years she had made a happy life for herself. But one day, when she was on the seashore, a band of slave traders kidnapped her and took her to Istanbul. For the second time, she had lost everything.

"A kindly man, a mast maker, took pity and bought her, thinking that perhaps her fortunes would be better if he, rather than someone else, did so. But when they returned to his home, they found his business in shambles. So he, his wife, and Fatima dedicated themselves to making ships' masts.

"Fatima worked so hard that she was granted her freedom. Once again she settled into a new life. Then one day, the mast maker said, 'Fatima, take these ships' masts to Java as my agent and sell them at a good price.' She set forth, but the ship was wrecked by a terrible typhoon off the coast of China (this girl could not get a break). She cursed and bewailed her fate that no matter how hard she tried, nothing ever worked out. 'Why am I jinxed?'

"What she couldn't have known was that in China there was a legend that one day an extraordinary woman would appear on the shore and build a marvelous building that no one had ever seen before, called a tent. From time to time the emperor of China would send scouts along the shore looking for this woman. One scout happened to be onshore when Fatima emerged from the sea, shaking her fist at God. And the scout said, 'You must come with me to the emperor's court.' When she arrived at the palace, the emperor said to her, 'Can you build this marvelous building we've heard so much about, called a tent?' Fatima, having seen many tents in her journeys, said, 'Of course.' 'Then do so,' said the emperor. 'First I'll need some stout cloth,' said Fatima. 'Ah, we have no such thing,' said the emperor. So Fatima remembered her time with the kindly Alexandrian weavers, and she wove the stout cloth herself. Then she said, 'Bring me some strong rope.' 'Ah, we have no such thing,' said the emperor. And she remembered her time with her father as a spinner, and she spun colorful stout rope. 'Now all I need,' she said, 'are long poles for the tent.' 'We have none of those,' said the emperor. And remembering her time making masts, she made the long posts.

"From all her careful observations of tents in all of her journeys, Fatima made the most marvelous tent that anyone had ever even imagined. And the emperor said, 'You have done this great thing. Name your reward.' She married a handsome prince, had children, and it was clear to her that each catastrophic chapter in her life had taught her something she needed to know to create her ultimate happiness."

WHAT DON'T I HAVE TIME TO THINK ABOUT?

It might be "Should I refinance the house?" or "Do I still love my partner?" Whatever it is, you can, if you wish, take this time to simply name it.

IS NOT HAVING TIME TO THINK ABOUT _____ CAUSING ANY PROBLEMS IN MY LIFE?

CQ appears with a soothing cup of tea. "Gal, the only way to build your life from the inside out is to stop, breathe, and check in. You can think about this issue if you let yourself settle in, if you remember that Ms. Anxiety is your buddy too, and if you stick with the silence for just a little while."

HOW CAN I NOURISH MYSELF?

CREATIVE EXPLORATION: Arrange flowers; create mail art from headlines, magazine clippings, old fortunes and horoscopes; or create a comfort scrapbook of things you love to do.

CULTURAL EXPERIENCE: AGE biography, special collections in a university library, book signing, opera, Kabuki, experimental theater; state fair to see the pigs . . .

FRIENDSHIP: Write postcards to five friends to thank them for a gift they've given you, even if it was a decade ago; break off a friendship that is no longer healthy . . .

Art from Scrap

I'm standing in the bathroom naked, about to step into the shower. I'm looking at myself in the two large mirrors that were supposed to make our tiny bathroom appear larger but only succeeded in doing so to me.

I study my knee, twice operated on, and my shoulder, once operated on, and my sinuses, also the recipient of unwanted surgical attention. I notice how I still lean to one side, favoring my weak knee.

The bathroom door opens a crack and a sign, hand-lettered in gold calligraphy, slides in. It reads, "Art from scrap." Either Lilly has learned to write overnight or CQ is up to her tricks again.

Looking in the mirror, I retort, "I thought you would say something like 'Love the one you're with.'"

"Same thing."

After my shower, I dress in my usual attire: loose drawstring pants that look suspiciously like plaid pajama bottoms and a white cotton T-shirt, this one only stained in two places.

Coming out of the bathroom, I find CQ making my bed. "What did you mean, art from scrap?"

"What are you going to make with what you've got? Like it or not, you're constrained by limits. These limits I'm talking about are not frames of mind, which can be overcome when the time is right and the will aligned (in other words, fierce desire engaged). Limits are the reality of who you are. You are a woman. You are a mother, a wife; you have a certain body, certain talents, a certain level of intelligence, a finite amount of energy. Some things are never going to change. To ignore this is to live in denial and miss where you are supposed to be."

I flop on the newly made bed. "This sounds so un-American. I'm sure Anthony Robbins and Stephen Covey are going to barge in here and have us arrested. I don't want to think about limits, I want to dream of unrestricted possibilities."

CQ lies down beside me. "Rabbi Akiba was a legendary first century Torah scholar," she says, her voice melodic and low. "He believed one of the Bible's principal messages was, 'Everything is fixed, but permission is given.' Think about last weekend when Chris and Lilly went away. You were so excited about having time to yourself, you imagined you were going to write for two and half days straight. What happened?"

"I got less than my usual amount of work done. In fact, I had a rather blah time. But that's what writers do: we wish for uninterrupted time and then we pluck our chin hairs."

"Besides the need for regular waxing, part of your problem is your unrealistic expectations," CQ reaches over and plucks a hair off my chin. Her technique is excellent, for it barely hurts. "You see you've adjusted to creating within the limits of your life: five hours of child care, constant interruptions, the sound of Chris's voice from his office. This helps you get your work done."

I extract *Flow* by Mihaly Csikszentmihalyi out of the tottering pile of books on my night table. "I read in here about a Professor Fausto Massimini who has studied paraplegics, mostly young people who've had accidents. And he found 'that a large proportion of the victims mentioned the accident that caused paraplegia as both one of the most negative and one of the most positive events in their lives. The reason tragic events were seen as positive was that they presented the victims with very clear goals while reducing contradictory and inessential choices. The patients who learned to master the challenges felt a clarity of purpose they had lacked before.'" I close the book. "Their physical limitations focused them, so they had to use more commitment and patience. One guy said he felt born again."

"Watch out. You're beginning to sound"—CQ does a perky imitation of a Junior Leaguer—"like it's simply super to be in a wheelchair."

"Of course not. It struck me that having limits or, better yet, recognizing limits, can help you create."

CQ looks around our half-remodeled bedroom. It has been half-remodeled for almost a year. "Limits do more than help you create; they give you the building blocks to create with. And the signposts. Limits are the form you pour yourself into."

I'm feeling uncomfortable. I lie still, breathing and following that feeling. "What about the billion people in the world who don't have running water, or the people in refugee camps or in abusive relationships, or children chained to rug looms? Are those limits making them more creative?" My voice has an edge to it.

CQ rolls over on her side and faces me. "Let me be very clear. Most people in the world cannot create their lives because they don't have enough to eat. Many people in the world are being exploited by gigantic international conglomerates that don't even answer to governments anymore. We do not create everything that happens in our lives. Each and every thing is not laid out in a preordained plan. To navigate by your limits, you have to learn to discern between societal injustices, beliefs, and limits. Limits are constraints you've been given to create within, elements like your temperament, your talents, your interests, your family, your intelligence. Beliefs are internal limits that you can work with, examine, and, if need be, replace. Societal injustices are limits slapped on you by an unjust and greedy world, and you must try to overcome those, for yourself and others. The doctor you mentioned before, Alison Eastbrook, the one who had all the trouble with her appointment to head the breast surgery department, that is a bogus limit placed on her by an asinine male world. She had to fight using her natural talents and within her limits. The woman in the refugee camp, is she there because of her limits? Probably not. But what can she make from it? How do you make something redemptive out of tragedy? How can you help others make something redemptive? We who have so much bear a responsibility to those who have nothing. A woman in an abusive relationship does not stay there and make art from her bruises, nor does she declare, 'I need to be here because this is my unfolding path.' That is masochistic fatalism. She can choose what meaning she finds in this abusive relationship. The fact that she stops and reflects is what is important. If she believes being abused is her destiny, she's given up."

"I think I understand," I say. "This is what I've got. What am I going to make with it?"

"Here is a limit: we each have twenty-four hours a day. We each have a finite amount of energy. The most basic way to create your life is to get to know that stream of energy and to take care of it. We are energetic beings. This is not spiritual rigmarole; this is science. We have to respect what our bodies are capable of. That means letting go of the stupefying unrealistic demands we put on ourselves. It can be something as basic as realizing you think things are going to take half the time they do, so you learn to put extra time into your schedule. It can be as basic as learning how much sleep you need."

"Women are going to throw this book across the room," I tell her. "They don't want to know how to do less; they want to know how to do more while feeling great."

"If you keep pushing and rushing to do the most you can in every moment, you will miss the life that truly fits you. You and many of the women you interviewed have experienced, over and over again, what happens to you when you ignore your physical limits. The only basis for creating your life, or at least the only way it's going to come to any kind of fruition—or as those New Agers like to say, manifestation—is to learn your limits and create within them."

"Name my limits."

"You need a certain amount of rest, time alone, and zealous exercise. You need to avoid certain foods. You have a young child, so you can only work so many hours a day. You have a certain level of education and brains. You carry a certain amount of shame, and your feelings are easily hurt. You need eight hours of sleep. I could go on."

I shake my head no. "I've heard enough. I get the idea."

"No, you haven't heard enough. You judge yourself for having these limits. Why? Your soul uses them to become what it is supposed to become. James Hillman said, 'You find your genius in the mirror of your life.' For some people, this is obvious. They have created a life that fits them by observing themselves. Other people haven't because they keep forcing themselves into what they think they should do, because their dad told them to, or what fools they would be if they didn't try to make a lot of money, or they compare themselves to the CEO who is worth a billion, has two kids, and is married to a brain surgeon, and they think, "Why not me?" Because that isn't your path. Look at your weaknesses and your limits not as shortcomings but as guideposts to aim between. You abandon your path when you focus on someone else's. Respect what your body is telling you and let it be the guide. Joy and satisfaction are the hallmarks of following your path, not money or esteem in other people's eyes."

I lie back on my pillow, exhausted after CQ's diatribe. I hated the idea of limits. Almost everything I had accomplished in my life seemed to be because someone said, "You can't."

This was tricky. What to accept and what to try to improve? I thought about Priscilla, who had told me, "I'm someone who doesn't fit the mold. I struggled a long time with that. During my college years and right after, I was discovering I didn't fit the mold. I didn't seem to fit the categories for how people live their lives, for how people work at their jobs. I plain didn't fit. Yet I could discover pieces of where I fit. I started stringing those together. There was the piece of working in a solitary cubicle, at an office or in the library, which I loved. That was one guideline I used to pursue the kinds of work I could do. That was a piece of my uniqueness. Another piece was that I'm not a nine-to-fiver. I could not keep my psychological health and hold to the schedule that almost everyone around me could hold to. It took me many years to accept that part of me. It's in the process of accepting parts of yourself that don't fit the norm that you find your uniqueness, that you find what makes you happy. Over those years, I discovered I had to be freelancer."

I thought about what James Hillman wrote about fate and fatalism in *The Soul's Code:* "Catching the sly wink of fate is a reflective act. It is an act of thought, while fatalism is a state of feeling, abandoning thoughtfulness, specific details, and careful reasoning. . . . Fatalism comforts, for it raises no questions. There's no need to examine just how events fit in." Instead Hillman cautions us to recognize that fate has only a "portion of our lives, calling them but not owning them." We identify the portion only by pondering, meditating, considering—listening. "Fate does not relieve me of responsibility; in fact, it calls for more."

I turn toward CQ, who is breathing deeply beside me. "I've always reached for what I wanted to accomplish, focusing on what was holding me back. I never thought to turn around and see if what was holding me back was pointing me in some better direction."

CQ concentrates for a moment before answering. "First, of course, you've got to accept and cherish your pesky, frisky limits. You've got to say, 'I am what I am,' and *love* it. That is so difficult. Most of us immediately spring to how we are going to change or fix ourselves. But what if you loved your limits and your flaws, really showered them with love, and only then asked them to direct you? What if you talked to your limits—to your food allergies, your exhaustion, your jitteriness, your dumbness, your impatience?" CQ grins. "Of course, to do any of this will require you to stop comparing yourself to others."

When she isn't looking, with one foot I clandestinely push an old copy of the *Wall Street Journal* under the bed. I had saved it to obsess over the story of Marlene Krauss, who in 1965 was among the first women to attend Harvard Business School. After a career on Wall Street, she decided she wanted to do something more humanitarian. She enrolled in Harvard Medical School at thirty, became an eye surgeon, married at thirty-nine, had a daughter at forty-four, then launched a health care venture-capital firm. She recently had twins at fifty-three.

"CQ, adult women don't do that kind of adolescent comparison shopping. We are completely beyond that."

We look at each other and burst out laughing.

WHAT IS ONE PERSONAL LIMIT I AM DENYING OR PUSHING RELENTLESSLY AGAINST?

Name one *wee* limit. Jennifer Freed said, "It took me a long time to figure out that I don't have consistent streams of energy. I have spurts, and then I have to lie down. When I was younger, I didn't pay attention to that, so I would get sick in order to take time off. Now I have to actually lie down to make sure I don't get sick. I know my cycle, and if I don't rest—it's a limitation, but if I work with it, it's almost a reality test. I don't feel victimized by it." For Anna, it was the limit of not making enough money to cover her monthly expenses.

WHERE IS THIS LIMIT TRYING TO POINT ME?

For Jennifer, toward rest. For Anna, the limit of her budget and the stress it produced pointed toward moving to a cheaper house or building up her nurse practitioner practice.

AM I ASKING FOR ENOUGH HELP IN MY LIFE?

Art from Scrap

Addenda

"You can go beyond many of your limits. You can have surgery to change the way you look or even your sex. You can go up in space and be free of gravity. You can diet for the rest of your life, work out for two hours a day, and have those cut abs everybody wants. You could go back to school to learn to read Proust." CQ jumps off the bed and stands over me. "But instead, try putting fierce desire, limits, and beliefs in a pot. Stir well, wait, watch, wait some more, and then see what rises to the surface. What do you need to push against and what do you need to go with? It takes vigilance, self-honesty, and a *lot* of checking in."

I get up to start a load of laundry, the laundry room being conveniently part of our bedroom. "You exhaust me. This is so much work."

With a low groan, CQ collapses on the bed. Worried, I rush over to her. She opens her eyes, and I see that she is crying. "You make this so much harder than it is. Stop fighting it. Stop trying to do it alone. You don't *have* to. Follow the *joy*. If you could only see yourself from where I sit. If you could only see what I see."

I look into her eyes, where black flecks form flowers around her pupils. I watch her crying for me, for my hardness, my austere, gritty, whiny, stubborn self.

I fall into her mercy.

WHAT CAN I DO TODAY WITH THE GIFTS THAT I HAVE?

Remember, this question focuses on what you can do and what you value, not on what you can't do or wish you could.

WHAT KIND OF CHANGES AM I SEEING IN MY DAILY LIFE BECAUSE OF MY INSIGHTS, YEARNINGS, AND INTENTION?

Look for subtle shifts, not lightning bolts. Where are the Aunties helping you?

WHAT DOES ONE RELATIONSHIP IN MY LIFE NEED THIS WEEK TO FLOURISH?

Attention	Gratitude	Letting go
Time together	Humor	Physical play
Third party to help us	Listening	Sharing nature
listen to each other	Sacrifice	Massage
Acceptance	The touch of the Divine	

Here are some more examples: By leaving a small basket with a tiny bar of soap, a sample of bath oil, a sachet, and a card, Sara nurtured her best friend, who was having a very hard week. Naomi sent three postcards to friends thanking them for gifts they had given her years ago, telling them how much she appreciated having those reminders of their love in her life. When Lilly asked me to play ball, instead of doing it for two minutes and making some excuse about how busy I was, I played with her until it got dark.

Fill in the blank: _____

A Window Opens
and God Breezes In

That night I lay in bed and thought about what CQ had said. I did make life harder than it needed to be. People had been telling me that my whole life. Follow the *joy.* Almost all writers write to discover themselves, "line by line as the words compose me," to quote memoirist Nancy Mairs. As I lay in bed and thought about my journey of the last year or so, I knew I had written this book for only one reason: to decide, question by question, if I could love myself.

True to form, CQ wasn't letting me off the hook. With her merciful tears, she had thrust my nose in it, exposed how I still hung on to my bundle of self-hatred.

Was I willing to give it up? Was I willing to follow the joy?

While I was in college, and for at least ten years afterward, I had a recurring nightmare about a faceless man in chains who would appear in my room. The room would be whatever room I was actually sleeping in, whatever apartment I was living in at the time, and I would feel awake, this faceless man coming out of the closet. I would scream, "He's really in here. He's really in here." Over the years I had been woken from the nightmare by my dad, my husband, the upstairs neigh-

bors, a police helicopter, and once, in Ireland, an entire youth hostel. The dream faded after I got pregnant, recurring every now and then as a force of choking blackness rushing at me.

Could I rid myself of even the rushing blackness? Or, better yet, learn from it? Could I transform my flinty belief that no matter what I did or thought or tried or wrote, I would never be enough? My friend recently fell in love. She said to me, with tears in her eyes, "He loves me so much. He thinks I'm the smartest, brightest, most wonderful person. How can he love me that much?" In her voice I felt the same catch, the same longing, that I felt in my own life. How could anyone love me that much—Chris, Lillian, my best friend Barbra, my sister, CQ?

I knew that, right now, the shelves of my study were crowded with books and tapes whose entire point was to help me love myself. I could hear Geneen Roth saying, "Your job is to do your best at all times. To be curious, to treat yourself with kindness, and to act on your own behalf." I could hear Thich Nhat Hanh's Vietnamese accent murmuring, "The capacity of listening to ourselves is the foundation of the capacity of listening to others. The capacity to love others depends on the capacity to love ourselves."

Shivering, I find the heating pad under the bed, turn it on, and position it under my feet. I pile on two more quilts. Upstairs, I hear Lilly moan in her sleep and I want to moan too.

I can feel the spot, the impenetrable hardness that skulks somewhere underneath my attempts to embrace life. I never quite get a good look at the blackness, the faceless man, but I can feel it there, weighing on me. I start to get up, turn on the light, and read a book, dodge this question, let it rest until another day. Then Marcie's words on the moss-encrusted trail echo through me: "It is what it is." I stop. Why run? I think. How much can this hurt? I've been here before. My fierce desire to create my life, to dig deeper than I have ever dug before, awakens. I breathe and remember my intention, the way I want to feel, alive and connected, intimate and loved. I try to conjure up those feelings, but all I can feel is my pulse thudding in my ears. I'm in a tiny submarine a mile under the ocean, and the pressure is beginning to crack the hull.

And what about faith?

I sit up to look for CQ but I don't see her. I hide under the covers. What about faith? I feel my calf muscles flexing against the duvet. Leap, girl.

Carry the darkness with you, my beloved, don't try to leave it behind. Pick it up, carry it with you, and still choose life. That is self-love. I peer under the covers for CQ even though I know she isn't there. I'm talking to myself the way she would talk to me.

Do you have the wherewithal, the courage, the stamina, to do what needs to be done? Look deeper, Jennifer, look there. What do you see?

I see myself walking down a long, dark hall and peering under the callused spot in my body where the darkness hides. With great effort, fighting sleepy gravity, I see myself facing the faceless man, the rushing blackness.

Shock waves of harshness rush at me; pellets of words sting my face; a rushing, barely perceivable montage of failings, of turning away from love, of judging others, flashes past, presses against me. I'm suffocating, it's too hard to breathe under this onslaught. Why am I doing this? My intention wavers, and immediately my panic ratchets up several notches. There is too much here for me to face. Too many failings. I see my mouth screaming at Lillian when she was a colicky baby. I see myself savoring my anger at Chris. And then a wave of boredom so dense and salty rises toward me and I start to turn away, gasping.

What about faith? I hear my voice ask. What about faith?

I remember I don't have to do this alone. I can choose to ask for help. With that thought, salty boredom turns to icy intellectual mockery. Faith, faith, faith howls past me like a vile curse.

What would CQ do? I ask myself, panicky. What would she do? Dance, girl. I would dance.

The howl becomes a roar. My breathing is rapid and shallow. This is a *big* creative moment, I think, and for some reason, that makes me giggle. And the giggle gives me just the moment of breathing room I need to imagine myself moving. To imagine myself swaying and gingerly lifting my feet, trying to find the rhythm of my grief. Any rhythm, somebody, can you give me a rhythm? A furious gust of awkward images of me dancing, from the sixth-grade dance to my wedding, all taken from a bad angle. I snatch the wedding image with my outstretched hand. I turn it until I can see the good angle, until I can see the love in my eyes. I hear the Strauss waltz we danced to. Then I really start to move. Head bent, arms outstretched, I listen to the rhythm inside me, I focus on that young face, so full of trust. I refuse to give in. I refuse to give in. I refuse to give in.

With each movement, the icy blasts become more bearable. With great effort, I raise my arms over my head, and in that rhythm, I find myself able to ask for help. It is not a whiny, desperate "Save me," not a child's plea but a woman's request for help seeing herself.

Somewhere down that long hall, a window opens. Just a crack. But enough for a clean breeze to blow in and caress my raised arms, my upturned hands, my bent head. The breeze caresses the darkness too, my icy fury, my inky failings. It fills our lungs, slows our breathing, and then it picks the darkness and me up. It picks us up and holds us close, mashed together, eye to eye.

I lie in the dark and breathe gingerly into the sensation of being one with this massive, unblinking darkness. I shiver, but this shiver is one of discovery, almost delight. With each breath, my feeling of delight and ease grows. Grows until I have to giggle. And my darkness almost giggles back.

Oh, so this is grace.

Lilly appears at the bedroom door. "Mommy," she breathes as she clambers down the steps and scrambles into bed. I turn down the covers for her. She touches my face and gives me a sleepy half-smile before collapsing onto her pillow and immediately falling back into her dense, sprawled sleep.

I watch her face by the dim glow of the night-light, now and then laughing a little and patting my dark spot, until I too fall asleep.

Living the Questions

39

WHAT HAVE I BEEN HOLDING AT THE EDGE OF MY MIND
THAT I WISH TO BRING INTO THE LIGHT?

Each time you ask yourself one of these questions, you sink deeper into your truth. Hard work but honest and required.

HOW CAN I INVITE THE LARGER ENERGIES—MYSTERY, DIVINE
INTELLIGENCE—INTO MY LIFE IN THE DAYS AHEAD?

Contemplate this question like a parable. Don't expect literal direction. Bring this question into your daily life.

IS THE RIVER MOVING?

Sufi poet Rumi said, "When you do things from your soul, you feel a river moving in you, a joy." Is that river moving in you right now?

Summer

Slow Down

Today is the first day of summer vacation for the kids in our neighborhood. Sitting outside on our back deck, eating breakfast, I can feel their elation, their freedom, as 8:20 passes and no bell rings from the school at the end of our street. I feel a bit of that same excitement, that same sort of glorious possibility stretching before me.

I found a note from CQ this morning, propped up next to my teapot. This is what it said: "Dear Jennifer. I'm off to do a little digging with Teilhard de Chardin. I'll be back if you need me. I've left you a few notes here and there because I know how you like plans and formulas, but as I think you learned last night, it really is very simple. Slow down. Breathe. Ask. Listen. Then throw it all away and walk into the fire, teeth gleaming. Love, CQ."

Listen

Teeth gleaming, I watch the wind in the trees.

WHAT IS THE ONE THING I NEED MOST IN MY LIFE RIGHT NOW?

Has what you need changed since you started this book? Has it shifted in some petite or giant way? CQ adds, "Are you letting yourself know what you really, really need most? Might as well. I promise, good things will come of it."

WHAT AM I WILLING TO ACCEPT ABOUT MYSELF,
AT LEAST IN THIS MOMENT, TRULY OPEN MY HEART AND ACCEPT?

One woman wrote, "My inability to love my stepdaughter as much as my daughter." Jan opened her heart to her ambition. Nikki named her inability to master a computer program at work. All the women found something that they could accept, for a moment, without trying to change or make deals with. Find that feeling, sit in the middle of it.

WHAT *ONE* THING COULD I DO IN THE DAYS AHEAD TO SUPPORT MY
BODY IN BEING PART OF THE CREATION OF MY LIFE?

One thing. Starting a whole new eating plan is too much. Eating one balanced breakfast of healthy fat, protein, nonstarchy veggies, and complex carbohydrates is perfect.

CQ's Cheat Sheet

CQ's cheat sheet will help you create your life on the days when you either are having too many "senior moments" or you simply need a handy refresher.

☆ Awareness is everything. Pay attention to your life. Ask yourself, "What's the next step? Do I push or do I let go? What direction are my character traits pointing me toward? What can I learn from how I am behaving?"

☆ Self-nurturing is not a reward, a goody, a little extra you give yourself because of all the crap you had to wade through: it is the ground of your being, the stuff with which you create your life. It is *attitude.*

☆ Live first by what you treasure.

☆ Help cannot come unless you ask. Imagine you hold a *celestial phone* card in your hand. The cost of using it is consciousness. Use it or lose it.

☆ The way you wish to feel in your life is the emotional blueprint you need to bring your mind back to, again and again. A mind without a focus is a rut.

☆ If you are stuck or in pain, stop. Breathe. Ask a question. Listen.

☆ Be open to the meaning in what you did not want to happen. Perhaps you are being pointed in a different direction, to expand your perceptions, or to meet a handsome stranger.

☆ Consider and welcome all the voices inside you. Don't judge or reject one in favor of the authentic voice. Listen with an open heart to all—but this never means act on what they say.

☆ The voices, ideas, and images you can trust resonate with the clarity of a single chime in perfect tune with your body.

- ✸ Revisit your insights and yearnings as often as you can. Ponder them like parables or koans. What do they reveal about you?
- ✸ Do not wait for life to get resolved. That day is never going to arrive. Stop wasting energy waiting and start leaping.
- ✸ Your perceptions, fears, and beliefs are obscuring your vision. They are invisible, and yet they block your way. We humans are creatures of habit. We get into and stay in ruts. Seeing those ruts is how you create your life. One way to see them is to rededicate yourself daily to taking responsibility for being the agent of your destiny. Don't wait, don't blame, don't worry.
- ✸ The anxious moment, the addictive moment, the controlling moment is also the greatest creative opportunity. It is the point between the halves of the hourglass. Each time it presents itself, you have another chance to choose wisdom and growth, to choose to be fully alive.
- ✸ Don't stop listening because things are cushy. God doesn't speak in money; she speaks in longing. Remain alert to the next prompting. Keep your eye on the unfolding path.
- ✸ Leap into believing you are enough. Soak in believing you are enough. Indulge in believing you are enough. Your sense of deserving will become as unshakable and as immutable as the earth.
- ✸ Listen to your fears of self-absorption and self-indulgence. What are they trying to tell you? Are they like the Wizard of Oz, hiding behind a curtain with no real power? Or are they messengers of change?
- ✸ The desire to create your life is based in self-kindness and fed by self-nurturing.
- ✸ You are not alone.
- ✸ Do not suffer needlessly by thinking you are.

CQ purrs in your ear as you settle in: "We're getting toward the end of our time together. What an amazing amount of energy you've given. I'm glowing with pride."

WHAT IS ONE LEAPING, TRANSFORMATIVE ACTION I COULD TAKE TO BREATHE FRESH INSPIRATION INTO MY LIFE?

Jan tried karate. Deborah started by buying one antique and reselling it on the Internet, working toward her dream of owning her own store.

Instead of _____, I could choose to _____.
Instead of _____, I could choose to _____.

Review your shadow comforts and time monsters. What might you choose differently in the near future?

HOW CAN I AWE AND ENTHRALL MY LIMITED, IMPERFECT, GLORIOUS SELF?

REVITALIZED RELATIONSHIP: What connection needs your love and attention? How will you give that attention in a way that serves the Divine and doesn't deplete you?

MIND CHALLENGE: Write your own crossword puzzle, take out the chessboard, read up on chaos theory, ponder Japanese art, learn to read ancient Greek, visit a section of the bookstore that you never venture into. . . .

Support for Being a Round Peg in a Square Hole

The more you create your life, the less you fit the life everybody else is living.

For years, I've traveled around the United States and even made a foray into Europe, and I've spotted us—women creating their lives from the inside out. We peek out from behind shopping carts and prams, from behind store counters and presidents' desks, from old and middle-aged faces, and occasionally young ones. We often waver and almost disappear again because it is so uncomfortable to wake up and look around. The injustices, greed, and the general state of the world weigh on us. It takes so much effort to remain a round peg, to be fully self-possessed.

Jennifer Freed told me how many women she sees in this bind: part of you wanting to turn within, part of you forever being seduced by the world. "There are so many women turning forty and fifty right now," she said. "I see half my clients and friends deciding to do inner work and the other half deciding to get face-lifts. It's going to be touch-and-go to see what wins out. What really makes you feel good about yourself? Inner work requires persistence because the outer culture doesn't support it, whereas trying to make yourself more appealing on the outside, the persona level, gets huge rewards—temporarily." It's not like this is a new struggle. It's just that the religious mystics of old weren't contemplating laser skin resurfacing. They had limited options.

"I suffer over this every day," my friend Deborah said on the phone when I called to talk about this duality. "I don't think that's such a bad thing, the suffering. My awareness is heightened and that can only be good. I'm not sure why enlightenment is better. I suppose because I'm gaining the right to choose."

I don't think the suffering is such a bad thing either (very Buddhist of me). The discomfort we are feeling is a grain of sand (granted, a big, harsh, *irritating* grain of sand) inside our oyster souls. We are being irritated into birthing fierce desire on a global level.

It's okay that we don't fit. It's scary and painful and, more often than not, a pain in the ass. That's okay. It helps a lot to know we are not alone. There are legions of women like you and me, Comfort Queens and Comfort Princesses and Comfort Crones, all of us creating our lives, spiral by spiral. Sherry Ruth Anderson and Paul Ray have named us Cultural Creatives, based on their ten years of survey-based research. They believe there are 48 million of us in the United States alone, women and men who have made a comprehensive shift in our worldview, embracing such values as the development of spirit, rejection of abject consumerism, development of meaningful relationships, political action, and love of nature, to name a few. When I heard Paul lecture, the point he stressed was that we don't believe there are so many of us out there. We feel isolated, working in small groups, unaware that there are enough of us to change the world.

Before you get overwhelmed, thinking I'm forming a new political party and asking you to be the campaign manager, all I want you to do for now is imagine, feel, drink in the fact that you are not alone. You may believe you are living your funky lifestyle with only the support of a few friends. You may believe that creating your life, listening, trying to be true to what you hear and feel, makes you wacky, weird, a granola-head. Nope. Not true. The wacky part might be true, but the alone part is not. There are millions of Cultural Creatives. Feel the filigree of women and men surrounding you who share your longing, your values, your courage. They get out of bed, rise from their futon, roll up their grass mats, leave their ship's berth, and meet the day as diligently, as imperfectly, as hopefully as you do.

Try this experiment. Buy a couple of packs of sticky dots from the office supply store, the kind you are supposed to use to identify files. I have a more subversive plan in mind. Take these dots with you, as you go about your business, and stick them here and there along the way. The bathroom at work, the spirituality section of the bookstore, by the organic cheese puffs in the health food store, in your child's school. The point? Perhaps in a few weeks or months, you will go back to one of those dots, spot it in passing, and there will be another dot keeping your dot company. Or perhaps you've have been seeing these dots around town and now you know what they mean.

Fellow mystics sending each other encouraging smoke signals.

WHERE DO I NEED SUPPORT IN SUSTAINING THE CREATION OF MY LIFE?
WHAT AREA, ATTITUDE, ACTION, NEEDS THE SHELTER
OF LIKE-MINDED SOULS?

CQ nods sagely, "You got to surround yourself with people who are working toward the same end, who declare, 'I am what I am' and 'It is what it is' and who will help you do the same."

WHAT INSIGHTS, YEARNINGS, AND INTENTIONS
DO I WANT TO CONTINUE WITH?

Revisit your cards. Rewrite them. Where have they shifted, been fulfilled, become boring or no longer relevant? What do you want to take with you? How will the Auntie Goals continue to guide you?

IF I HAD TO CONDENSE INTO ONE OR TWO LINES THE MESSAGE I'VE BEEN SENDING THE UNIVERSE WHILE WORKING WITH THIS BOOK, WHAT WOULD THOSE LINES BE?

TIME FOR ONE LAST SNAPSHOT OF THE HEART.
WHAT DO I WANT TO REMEMBER FROM THIS
PROCESS? WHAT MOMENT DO I WANT TO HOLD
CLOSE TO MY HEART TO KEEP ME INSPIRED TO
CONTINUE THE WORK OF LIVING MY LIFE
FROM THE INSIDE OUT?

Living the Questions

continued

WHAT PART OF THE PROCESS OF WORKING WITH THIS BOOK
DO I NEED TO LET MYSELF OFF THE HOOK FOR, FLUSH THE GUILT AWAY,
FORGIVE MYSELF?

Do not—I repeat: *do not*—leave this book with any vestiges of "I should have done this," feelings of failings or perfectionism. You are enough. There is no right way. CQ shouts from your rooftop, "There is no one way!"

Remain alert to the next prompting!

Here

When I finished my last book, *The Woman's Retreat Book,* I remember slipping off the kitchen bar stool where I had just dotted the last *i* on my final edit, and as I stood up, I had the distinct feeling something fell off me–*plunk!* Ended. Done. Come full circle. It took three years to hear what that feeling of completion meant, to follow it to here.

Where is here? Not where my dramatic fantasies thought it would be. House gone, living in an RV, slinging hamburgers to pay the bills. The outside of my life doesn't look that different: I'm still married, still a mom, still learning to live in the perpetual transition that defines freelance work. Getting to here has been very gradual, an inside job.

I'm leaping forward with faith that my next step will be revealed.

That's what you have to keep doing too. You can start over with the questions in this book; you can use them over and over again. Or maybe it is time to write your own questions, to create your own spiritual day planner. The only thing that matters is that you keep being aware.

And that you reward yourself for making it through this process. Here's an idea: go on a retreat (I can recommend a great book to help you), even for an hour, and look back over this book. Perhaps take your conventional date book or calendar along. Start at the date in which you began responding to this book, writing this letter to yourself. Let yourself glide over memories of the past months or years. What moments can you pinpoint in which you reacted differently? Where did you find yourself living from the inside out? Look for the moments of self-kindness. Perhaps you've experienced a dramatic shift, the quitting of a job or the starting of a new one, having a baby, falling in love, creating a work of art. That's grand.

Remember also to peer into the corners of your life, searching for delicate changes in attitude and atmosphere. Watch for the spiral turns, for the places you've begun to see things from a slightly different direction.

As you do, you might stop for a moment to admire your crown.

We stand together, circles and circles of women, interwoven. Adjusting the weight of our crowns as we navigate the middle way between self-acceptance and denial, between developing our passions and serving the greater whole, between creating our lives and letting our lives create us.

Naomi Newman gives us her own cheat sheet in *Snake Talk:* "You dig, you bend down, you throw away, you go in circles, you get lost, you wait, you listen, you do nothing. You fall-down-you-get-up and inside you unfold. That's it in a nut-shell."

We link hands. We are not alone. We have each other.

Namasté.

Appendix

I extend a humble thank-you to these authors whose ideas and stories inform this book.

Are You Somebody: An Accidental Memoir by Nuala O'Faolain (New York: Henry Holt, 1996).

The Art of Happiness: A Handbook for Living by His Holiness the Dalai Lama and Howard C. Cutler, M.D. (New York: Riverhead Books, 1998).

Balancing Heaven and Earth: A Memoir of Visions, Dreams, and Realizations by Robert Johnson with Jerry M. Ruhl (San Francisco: Harper San Francisco, 1998).

The Bond Between Women: A Journey to Fierce Compassion by China Galland (New York: Riverhead Books, 1998).

Callings: Finding and Following an Authentic Life by Gregg Michael Levoy (New York: Crown Publishers, 1997).

Coming Home to Myself: Reflections for Nurturing a Woman's Body and Soul by Marion Woodman with Jill Melnick (Berkeley: Conari Press, 1998).

Composing a Life: Life as a Work in Progress by Mary Catherine Bateson (New York: Penguin Books, 1990).

Contentment: A Way to True Happiness by Robert Johnson and Jerry M. Ruhl (San Francisco: Harper San Francisco, 1999).

Dance of the Spirit: The Seven Steps of Women's Spirituality by Maria Harris (New York: Bantam Doubleday Dell Publishers, 1991).

Divided Lives: The Public and Private Struggles of Three American Women by Elsa Walsh (New York: Anchor Books/Doubleday, 1996).

Divine Daughters: Liberating the Power and Passion of Women's Voices by Rachel Bagby (San Francisco: Harper San Francisco, 1999).

Enduring Grace: Living Portraits of Seven Women Mystics by Carol Flinders (San Francisco: Harper San Francisco, 1993).

Fearless Creating: A Step-by-Step Guide to Starting and Completing Your Work of Art by Eric Maisel, Ph.D. (New York: Tarcher/Putnam, 1995).

The Feminine Face of God: The Unfolding of the Sacred in Women by Sherry Ruth Anderson and Patricia Hopkins (New York: Bantam Doubleday Dell Publishing, 1991).

Fire With Fire by Naomi Wolf (New York: Random House, 1993).

Flow: The Psychology of Optimal Experience by Mihaly Csikszentmihalyi (New York: Harper-Collins, 1991).

The Gastronomical Me by M.F.K. Fisher (New York: North Point Press, 1989).

Going to Pieces Without Falling Apart: A Buddhist Perspective on Wholeness by Mark Epstein (New York: Broadway Books, 1998).

The Heart Aroused: Poetry and the Preservation of the Soul in Corporate America by David Whyte (New York: Bantam Doubleday Dell Publishing, 1994).

Home: The Making of Sanctuary (audio) by Gunilla Norris (Boulder, Colo.: Sounds True, 1995).

Independent Women: Creating Our Lives, Creating Our Visions by Debra Sands Miller (Berkeley: Wildcat Canyon Press, 1998).

In Their Own Words (audio; Boulder, Colo.: Sounds True, 1999). This tape contains interviews with spiritual teachers and includes a Thich Nhat Hanh lecture from which I quoted on page 9.

The Invitation by Oriah Mountain Dreamer (San Francisco: Harper San Francisco, 1999).

Letter to Earth by Elia Wise (New York: Harmony Books, 2000).

A Life of One's Own by Joanna Field (New York: J.P. Tarcher, 1981).

Listening to the Oracle: The Ancient Art of Finding Guidance in the Signs and Symbols All Around Us by Dianne Skafte, Ph.D. (San Francisco: Harper San Francisco, 1997).

Live the Life You Love: In Ten Easy Steps by Barbara Sher (New York: Bantam Doubleday Dell Publishers, 1997).

Making the Gods Work for You: The Astrological Language of the Psyche by Caroline W. Casey (New York: Harmony Books, 1998). The story of Fatima is interpreted from Caroline's interpretation of a story from Idries Shah's book *Tales of the Dervishes* (New York: E.P. Dutton, 1969).

The New American Spirituality: A Seeker's Guide by Elizabeth Lesser (New York: Random House, 1999).

Ordinary Time: Cycles in Marriage, Faith and Renewal by Nancy Mairs (Boston: Beacon Press, 1994).

Reinventing Womanhood by Carolyn G. Heilbrun (New York: W.W. Norton & Company, 1979).

At the Root of This Longing: Reconciling a Spiritual Hunger with a Feminist Thirst by Carol Lee Flinders (San Francisco: Harper San Francisco, 1998).

The Seven Spiritual Laws of Success: A Practical Guide to the Fulfillment of Your Dreams by Deepak Chopra (Amber-Allen Publishers, 1995).

Silence: Making the Journey to Inner Quiet by Barbara Erakko Taylor (Philadelphia, Pa.: Innisfree Press, 1997). The story on page 177 is adapted with permission from pages 83–87.

Singing at the Top of Our Lungs: Women, Love and Creativity by Claudia Bepko and Jo-Ann Krestan (New York: HarperCollins, 1993).

Snake Talk by Naomi Newman (video of Naomi's play produced by the Traveling Jewish Theater; to order, write PO Box 421985, San Francisco, CA 94142).

The Soul's Code: In Search of Character and Calling by James Hillman (New York: Random House, 1996).

The Spell of the Sensuous by David Abram (New York: Vintage Books, 1996).

Survival Stories edited by Kathryn Rhett (New York: Anchor Books/Doubleday, 1997).

There Are No Accidents by Robert Hopcke (New York: Riverhead Books, 1997).

Things Seen and Unseen: A Year Lived in Faith by Nora Gallagher (New York: Alfred. A Knopf, 1998).

Transitions: Making Sense of Life's Changes by William Bridges (New York: Addison-Wesley Publishing, 1980).

The Way of Woman: Awakening the Perennial Feminine by Helen M. Luke (New York: Doubleday, 1995).

When the Heart Waits: Spiritual Direction for Life's Sacred Questions by Sue Monk Kidd (San Francisco: Harper San Francisco, 1990).

When Things Fall Apart: Heart Advice for Difficult Times by Pema Chodron (Boston and London: Shambhala, 1997).

When Work Doesn't Work Anymore: Women, Work, and Identity by Elizabeth Perle McKenna (New York: Bantam Doubleday Dell Publishing, 1997).

When You Eat at the Refrigerator, Pull Up a Chair: 50 Ways to Feel Thin, Gorgeous, and Happy (When You Feel Anything But) by Geneen Roth (New York: Hyperion, 1998).

A Woman on Paper: Georgia O'Keeffe by Anita Pollitzer (New York: Simon & Schuster, 1988).

A Woman's Book of Life: The Biology, Psychology, and Spirituality of the Feminine Life Cycle by Joan Borysenko, Ph.D. (New York: Riverhead Books, 1998).

Your Best Year Yet: A Proven Method for Making the Next Twelve Months the Most Successful Ever by Jinny S. Ditzler (New York: Warner Books, 1994).

From the Author

Please contact me. Hearing from readers keeps me going and inspires my books. I would be honored to hear stories of your Comfort Queen and about how you create your life, for possible inclusion in future projects and on my Web site.

www.comfortqueen.com is a daily living site that is like walking into your best friend's house, collapsing onto her fluffy couch, knowing she has just what you need to make you feel better: inspirational advice, comforting ideas and even a few goodies. Come subscribe to our Comfort Queen newsletter, see our spiritual time management on-line reminders, and learn about my speaking schedule.

Or send a self-addressed stamped envelope to PO Box 3584, Santa Barbara, CA, 93130, and I will send you info and a firefly of comfort.

And look for the Comfort goods—cards, notecards, journals, prints, teapots, mugs, magnets, frames, calendars, and more—with art by Cleo Papanikolas (she illustrated this book) and inspiration by me. For years readers asked me to do comfort goodies. I finally decided to go for it because I met Cleo, an incredible painter who had been painting images of comfort at the same time I was writing about it, and because I realized we all need reminders (me, most of all!). What better way to remind ourselves to use self-nurturing to become whole and powerful than by weaving the messages into the things we look at and use every day?

I hope to hear from you soon.